EXPERIENCE THE MYSTERY

EXPERIENCE THE MYSTERY

Pastoral Possibilities for Christian Mystagogy

David Regan

A Liturgical Press Book

 THE LITURGICAL PRESS
Collegeville, Minnesota

Published in North America by The Liturgical Press, Collegeville, Minnesota
Published in Great Britain by Geoffrey Chapman, a Cassell imprint

First published 1994

Library of Congress Cataloging-in-Publication Data
Regan, David, 1926–
    Experience the Mystery: pastoral possibilities for Christian mystagogy / David Regan.
      p.   cm.
    Revision of doctoral thesis – Pontifical Gregorian University at Rome, 1992.
    Includes bibliographical references and index.
    1. Mystagogy – Catholic Church.   2. Pastoral theology – Catholic Church.   3. Catholic
    Church – Clergy.   4. Initiation rites – Religious aspects – Catholic Church.   5. Catholic
    Church – Liturgy.   6. Spiritual formation – Catholic Church.   7. Catholic Church –
    Doctrines.   I. Title.
    BX1913.R636 1994   94–384
    253–dc20   CIP

ISBN 0–8146–2328–X

Cover illustration: William Blake, *The Ascent of the Mountain of Purgatory*.
© Tate Gallery, London. Photograph by John Webb.

Typeset by Litho Link Ltd, Welshpool, Powys, Wales
Printed and bound in Great Britain by Mackays of Chatham PLC

CONTENTS

FOREWORD

Religion is not exclusively, nor in the first place, something intellectual: it is an experience of God, and, for the Christian, an experience of the central Mystery of Christ.

I recall that in the Church this view of religion has always had a place. In 1259, in spite of the growing strength of the more rational Aristotelian attitude to theology, St Bonaventure wrote his *Itinerarium mentis in Deum*, in defence of the primacy of experience of God in the theological process.

Mystagogy is an ancient and traditional means of giving effect to this intuition. In mystagogy the candidate is initiated into an experience of the Christian Mystery. The contribution of the Fathers to making mystagogy part of Christian initiation was enormous: Cyril of Jerusalem in particular.

To wish to give mystagogy a larger place in pastoral action is opportune.

I am happy to make this thesis my own.

Paulo Evaristo, Cardinal Arns
Archbishop of São Paulo, Brazil

ABBREVIATIONS

AG	*Ad Gentes*: Vatican II, Decree on the Church's Missionary Activity
CT	*Catechesi Tradendae*: On Catechesis, Pope John Paul II, 1979
DTC	*Dictionnaire de Théologie Catholique*
DV	*Dei Verbum*: Vatican II, Dogmatic Constitution on Divine Revelation
EN	*Evangelii Nuntiandi*: Apostolic Exhortation, Pope Paul VI, 1975
GS	*Gaudium et Spes*: Vatican II, Pastoral Constitution on the Church in the Modern World
ICEL	International Commission on English in the Liturgy
Kittel	G. Kittel and G. Friedrich (eds), *Theological Dictionary of the New Testament*, English trans., 10 vols (Grand Rapids: Eerdmans, 1964–76); abridged in 1 vol. (Grand Rapids: Eerdmans/Exeter: Paternoster, 1985)
LG	*Lumen Gentium*: Vatican II, Dogmatic Constitution on the Church
LMD	*La Maison-Dieu*
NA	*Nostra Aetate*: Vatican II, Declaration on the Relation of the Church to Non-Christian Religions
NRT	*Nouvelle Revue Théologique*
Puebla	Documents of the Third General Conference of the Latin American Episcopate, 1979, English trans. (Maryknoll, NY: Orbis)
PUG	Pontificia Universitas Gregoriana, Rome
RCIA	*Ordo initiationis christianae adultorum* (Rite of Christian Initiation of Adults), 1972
REB	*Revista Eclesiástica Brasileira* (quarterly; Petrópolis, RJ, Brazil)
RM	*Redemptoris Missio*: Encyclical Letter of Pope John Paul II, 1990
SC	*Sacrosanctum Concilium*: Vatican II, Constitution on the Liturgy
SEDOC	*Serviço de Documentação* (bimonthly; Petrópolis, RJ, Brazil)
TS	*Theological Studies*
UR	*Unitatis Redintegratio*: Vatican II, Decree on Ecumenism
USCC	United States Catholic Conference, Inc.

ACKNOWLEDGEMENTS

Thanks are due to Fr Bruno Secondin OCarm of the Spirituality Department in the Gregorian University, Rome, Director of the thesis which underlies this book. He first sparked off work on the theme of mystagogy.

John B. Doyle of Ji-Paraná, Rondônia, Brazil, read the final text and made suggestions, applying, to good effect, what a mutual friend has called his 'crap detector'. My sincere thanks for his generosity.

The Experience of God by Dermot Lane, Copyright © 1981. First published by Veritas Publications, is used with permission.

INTRODUCTION

What is mystagogy? The word itself has not become accepted into the vocabulary of educated Catholics; if most clerics and religious have ever heard it, they have no idea what it means, and yet it is not more difficult, nor more Greek, than Eucharist, kerygma (which has returned to use in recent decades), ecclesiology, theology or pedagogy. It is an old word, coming from pre-Christian religions, borrowed from them by the early Church, then forgotten for centuries but officially revived in 1972.

Mystagogy is that which leads newcomers into an experience of mystery. Experience rather than intellectual knowledge is its keynote. The mystagogic is an approach to religious education that stresses the experiential. In this it provides a necessary counterbalance to an exclusively doctrinal catechesis. It was John Wesley who said that the intellectual theology and style of preaching of the Christian Churches of his time was quite incapable of producing conversions. History has proved the truth of his judgement, since the alienation of the working class from the mainline Churches, already causing preoccupation in his day, has become general all over Europe. The 'working class', not to speak of the growing unemployed class, has been joined by most of the other classes in finding preaching and religious education irrelevant to the world of their experience.

Attempts to create new and less intellectual forms of religious formation spread apace. It is surprising that the movements which engage in this pastoral activity, several of which use terms from the classical period of the Christian initiation of adults, have not discovered mystagogy. The European attempt to revitalize the faith of those baptized in infancy but grown indifferent is called by the name of 'catechumenate'. This use scarcely accords with the traditional meaning of the term. 'Mystagogy' would be a less inaccurate expression and an approach more likely to produce the hoped-for fruit.

Publication of the new *Catechism of the Catholic Church* has given rise to questioning of the value of a uniform catechesis in a pluricultural world. Occasionally bishops and priests speak of Tridentine catechesis as though it were the only solidly grounded and traditional approach to religious formation known to the Church throughout its history. Sometimes advocates of doctrinal catechesis decry any alternative approach which takes account of religious experience or the affective side of life. These, it is implied, are modern, suspect and sure to amount to an ephemeral fashion, in vogue today and gone tomorrow, while the learning of doctrine will last. Without creating an either/or polarization, it is opportune to recall the ancient and traditional pastoral practice of Christian mystagogy which is primarily geared to leading men and women to *experience* the central mystery of their faith. It is misleading to say that the 'traditional' form of religious education in the Church is catechetical and primarily intellectual. Mystagogy, centred on experience of the divine, is equally ancient.

Mystagogy, with emphasis on the central Mystery of Christ, provides the corrective desired by those who think that theological and liturgical renewal have 'taken mystery out of religion'; it makes experience of that Mystery the hub of Christian initiation. Clearly focusing Christian vision on the one Mystery of Christ, mystagogy also corrects the distortion which looked on facets of Christian truth as distinct 'mysteries of faith', splintering the splendid whole into fragments.

The renewal brought about by the biblical, patristic and liturgical movements, and especially by Vatican II, re-established the Paschal Mystery of Christ as the centre of Christian faith. Mystagogy, always directed towards initiation into *the* mystery, finds itself at home once more in this unified theological climate. Here mystagogy can grow and produce abundant fruit, while more recent plants are withering.

This book is written out of the conviction that mystagogy is a precious pastoral tool that has been largely overlooked if not forgotten. It is pastoral agents who must be convinced that mystagogy is a traditional pastoral practice whose time has come again. Once the pastoral agents see the importance and value of mystagogy for their task, the academic and publishing communities can be relied on to provide the scholarly material to back up the pastoral intuition.

By 'pastoral' is understood the Church's action towards the realization of the mission confided to it by Jesus Christ. Place and time are co-ordinates of this pastoral task. It deals with concrete measures for the conversion of men and women and the transformation of the world in each particular place and time. The application of the love of Christ to men and women of today in the changing circumstances of contemporary life is its scope. The better to do this, pastoral action, and the planning which precedes it, employ the social sciences to gain an objective picture of the world which it aims at influencing by the power of the Gospel. Theology as a whole is coming to resemble the pastoral process, in starting from concrete situations, which are then read in the light of faith so as to arrive at decisions for action to change whatever is seen as distant from the utopia of the Kingdom of God. Conversion as preparation for the coming of the Kingdom was central to Jesus' preaching (Matt 4:17; Mark 1:14–15). It was its practical aim, calling for relevance on the part of the Church's approach to men and women of today's world, which gave to the Second Vatican Council its title of a Pastoral Council, and to its most typical document that of the Pastoral Constitution on the Church in the Modern World, *Gaudium et Spes*.

Based on a doctoral thesis, presented at the Pontifical Gregorian University in Rome, in 1992, this study forgoes scholarly apparatus in order to make its pastoral appeal more direct. Enough references have been retained to show that there does exist some bibliography on mystagogy and that the arguments adduced in these pages are not a web of homespun fantasy.

I taught liturgy at senior seminary level in the 1950s, and at theology faculty level in the 1980s. The intervening years I spent as pastor in a large parish and then in pastoral co-ordination at diocesan and national levels in Brazil, where I now teach theology at postgraduate level. This varied pastoral experience has helped me appreciate the singular treasure of mystagogy which still remains largely buried. I think it worth the effort to make it better known, not just historically, but in terms of its pastoral efficacy for today.

Liturgical studies had made me aware of the ancient practice of mystagogy, but it was several decades later, while engaged in the study of missiology, in Rome, that mystagogy was drawn to my attention once more. For this I have to thank Father Bruno Secondin OCarm, Professor at the School of Spirituality in the Pontifical Gregorian University. In a course taught by him on 'Movements, Groups and Communities in the Church', he assigned, as a theme for a term paper, the task of describing the mystagogy of the movement, group or community of one's choice. I chose to work on 'The mystagogy of basic ecclesial communities in Brazil'. At first, it proved difficult to find anything at all written on mystagogy, but gradually a modest bibliography emerged.

No comprehensive work exists on the topic of mystagogy as a whole. There is a fair bibliography on patristic mystagogy; a growing literature, especially in France, on the liturgical revival of mystagogy; and a modest but valuable number of works, in Italy, on mystagogy as applied to spiritual life and direction. Nowhere have I come across any attempt to treat of all brands of mystagogy as a coherent whole and to apply the results to contemporary pastoral needs.

Mystagogy did not begin with the Christian Fathers. It began with the traditional religions of Greece and Rome and it was due to the inculturating genius of fourth-century pastors that the language and practice of mystagogy became, for a short few centuries, a vital aspect of Christian religious formation. Its wider human, extra-Christian origins entitle us to be freer in our use of the categories of mystagogy than if it had been an exclusively Christian creation. What the Fathers did for pastoral motives, in borrowing an experience-oriented approach to religious initiation, employed by the traditional religions of their time, we may do today when human and religious initiation are once more valued. Mystagogy was not a Christian invention but a borrowing from the worldwide, human practice of initiation. We are not limited to the particular style of borrowing done by our fourth-century predecessors in the art of Christian initiation.

The early Christian tradition on mystagogy reminds us that prior to an intellectualizing of theology there existed a holistic approach to the transmission of Christian faith. It is traditional, in the best sense of the word, to wish to have once again a religious education wider in scope than the learning of truths. A deeper and more totally human approach existed for centuries and is associated with names such as Cyril of Jerusalem, Ambrose of Milan, John Chrysostom (from Antioch) at Constantinople, all pastors of venerable memory and with experience of important sees.

The death of rural cultures in First World countries, paralleled and partly provoked by urbanization, has exposed young people to sophisticated specialization without the apprenticeship in growth provided by parents and the extended family in a farming community, or by the elders in a simpler urban setting. Initiation is lacking, leaving generations with hard work ahead to catch up with a maturity their elders grew into more naturally.[1] The work of Christian initiation could be total and could provide the psychic substratum for a full person, while opening up the deeper reaches of the Christian Mystery in which all life finds new meaning. Those who provide the means and occasions for this growth to Christian adulthood would be mystagogues.

Scholastic theology, a brilliant success during the Middle Ages and for some time after, was propped up by authority long after a changing society had rendered it intellectually obsolete. Based on Greek philosophy, for which things material, history and change were not matter for scientific reflection, Scholasticism has proved bankrupt in the face of the great problems of our age. For these it cannot offer ways of approach, much less answers; its ahistorical genius is at a loss in dealing with history and problems arising from technological change. With the Second Vatican Council, the Catholic Church began, perilously late in the day, to face up to the theological problems raised by the Reformers, by the advent of modern science and by the end of the colonial era. During the centuries since the Council of Trent, the problems of the modern world had been swept under the convenient carpet of condemnation. New ways of doing theology were needed and experimentation began. The shelving of the thousand-year-old Scholasticism left perplexity in the minds of many clerics, religious educators and thoughtful laity.

The rise of new theologies, each dealing with a problematic aspect of the historical scene: Feminist Theology, Theology of Liberation, Black Theology . . . has offered pluralism where before a monolithic system prevailed. Some people have been unable to understand the change of perspective and, perplexed at what appears as indefinition in theology, have turned to mysticism. They have wisely gone deeper than the theological, to try to experience God in the darkness of faith, because intellectual attempts to speak of things religious left them dissatisfied. Books and courses on mysticism abound. New works are published and the classics on Christian mysticism re-edited. Retreats and prayer groups cater for an increasing number who adhere to or show interest in pre-Christian or extra-Christian forms of cosmological mysticism and the genre spills over into diverse forms of mythology and magic. Oriental varieties of mysticism, in theory and practice, are popular and have helped change the lives of many.

In this religious climate, Christian mystagogy, which seeks to lead to God through experience, has much to offer. It has the advantages of being an early Christian pastoral art and of having roots in the worldwide traditional, human and religious practice of initiation. For Christians sensitive to contemporary culture it can provide an authentic approach to religious experience which has not, in fact, been provided either by liturgy or by standard religious formation.

The first chapter of this book looks at the early history of mystagogy in the mystery religions of Greece and Rome and gives a brief account of the way in which, beginning in the fourth century, the practice was borrowed by bishops of the Christian Church. Chapter 2 describes the recovery of mystagogy in our time, as part of the setting up of a real catechumenate as ordered by Vatican II. Here, as well as looking at the official, liturgical recovery of the practice, I describe two other uses of the language of mystagogy – by Karl Rahner and by theologians of spirituality. The third chapter shows how the element of experience (of the divine, in this case), which is central to mystagogy, is also typical of the contemporary 'culture of experience', making the return of mystagogy opportune. Chapter 4 deals with the place of the Word of God in mystagogy. Chapters 5 and 6 describe two sides of the classical context in which Christian mystagogy introduces neophytes to an experience of the Mystery: liturgy and community. Chapter 7 looks at the Mystery which mystagogy is to help candidates experience. Initiation to adult Christian living is explored in Chapter 8, as is the issue of inculturation, which is called for when men and women have to live Christian faith in new cultural circumstances – mystagogy, involving experience, cannot avoid dialogue with the culture which mediates that experience. Bound up with Christian initiation, mystagogy is closely related to religious formation; Chapter 9 considers the changes needed in formation if the mystagogic approach to becoming adult Christians is to be taken seriously. The final chapter recalls the objective of Christian life – service of the Christian and wider community – and outlines the role of the Spirit in mystagogy.

Tried and long valued in the Church, mystagogy has its place carved out alongside parallel structures of evangelization and catechesis, each of which it influenced in early times. It only remains to give it once more the place so obviously waiting for it today. That place must be in part created, as a new pastoral practice alongside those already occupying the field. In part it must be discovered already existing: by catechists who have long been trying to provide an experience of Christ parallel to and ahead of the imparting of doctrine; by chaplains and spiritual directors of religious groups and movements, who strive to show their members the way into the depths of the Mystery at the centre of their prayer and apostolic activity; by animators of basic communities who are aware of the value for the construction of the Kingdom of the change in economic, political and social structures aimed at by the communities. This opening of minds and hearts to the existence of a facet of Christian living specifically oriented towards experience of the central Mystery of Christ is rather more than helping men and women discover, like Molière's character, that they have been 'speaking prose all their lives'. The rediscovery of mystagogy draws attention once again explicitly to the vital element of religious experience so long marginalized by theology, thus reinforcing this element in religion. This underlining of the role of mystagogy, and the religious experience to which it draws attention, allows of the reuniting of spirituality (and mysticism) with theology and with pastoral action, healing a 1,500-year-long rupture, so that the rediscovery brings something new onto the horizon of faith.

Once basic awareness of the power of mystagogy is achieved, pastoral structures to set that spiritual energy to work will spring up overnight. It would be premature of me to do more than make tentative suggestions as to the shape such structures might take. If this leaves the legitimate appetite for concrete examples of mystagogy at work unsatisfied, the condition is inevitable in the present situation. Colourful details of mystagogy at work must await recognition of the potential of this pastoral practice in a variety of pastoral situations. This study aims at promoting such recognition. In the text, most examples are taken from the new and concrete pastoral structure of basic ecclesial communities. This choice of example is meant to combat any notion that mystagogy belongs to a disincarnate and 'spiritualized' Christianity.

Where does mystagogy belong theologically? Its keynote of religious experience – something essential to spirituality and starting-point for pastoral reflection – provides a sense of direction in any search for a home for mystagogy. Experience is the element which recommends the practice of mystagogy to pastoral concern, and if experience is more difficult to analyse than theological statements, it has more potential for uniting. The human personality can find in experience an integration which is sought in vain in ideas and a haphazard group can become a community through common religious experience – this latter is the story of so many basic ecclesial communities.

What department in theology should provide a course on mystagogy? Current experience of a theology faculty shows that the question is not a hypothetical one. Being a multidisciplinary theme, it is not at once obvious to what branch of ecclesiastical studies mystagogy belongs. The chapter headings of this book suggest some of the areas of theology to which mystagogy is related: liturgy is the obvious one; 'experience' and 'initiation' carry pastoral implications; consideration of the Mystery of Christ brings in systematic theology; the origins of Christian mystagogy involve patristics; the more recent history of the term makes it of interest to spiritual theology; the relation of mystagogy to catechetics makes the topic relevant to religious formation; and the whole history of mystagogy points it towards missiology – the initiation of candidates to the Christian community and Mystery. While to the academic this pluridimensional richness may constitute a weakness, it is one of the strengths of mystagogy that it introduces a unity into theology. It points theology once more in the direction of its centre, correcting the centrifugal tendency of the intellectual analysing typical of Scholasticism. Mystagogy is capable of uniting theology (in the narrow sense of an intellectual exercise), spirituality and the practical arts of pastoral and mission action. The central preoccupation of the Christian Church, which is the pastoral one, embraces experience alongside knowledge, at the service of its mission. Following the central intuition which led to Vatican II, pastoral concern must unite all ecclesiastical disciplines: theology, spirituality and religious formation, in seeking a common aim at the service of the men and women of our time. In this unified effort mystagogy must have its place.

The experiential, holistic and Mystery-centred characteristics of mystagogy remind us of its dependence on the Spirit. The Spirit is behind genuine religious experience, inspires unity and makes the Mystery operative – in Christ and in his Church. Mystagogy, like the Spirit, belongs to the practical order, eludes categorizing and is capable of pervading many aspects of Christian life. If such a discreet, yet all-pervading role makes mystagogy resemble the Spirit, perhaps that is why mystagogy has been invisible to the Church during so many centuries – so was the Spirit.

Most of the studies on mystagogy that I have seen are published in French, Italian or German, with a smaller number in Portuguese or Spanish. With the exception of Rahner's essays and the book by E. Mazza, on the theology of liturgy,[2] little of the relevant material has been translated into English. With the exception of Rahner, it is only since the 1970s that mystagogy has attracted attention and led to the publication of some initial studies.[3] The quantity of the published material is still small.

When this work was receiving its final touches, a study appeared which could not be ignored. It was the collection of papers presented at the 39th Saint-Serge Liturgical Study Week, held in Paris in 1992, and published in July 1993, under the title *Mystagogie: pensée liturgique d'aujourd'hui et liturgie ancienne* ('Mystagogy: Liturgical Thinking Today and in Ancient Times').[4] It is one of the most important publications on mystagogy to date.[5] The volume brought useful corrections in perspective (especially to one who is not a patristic scholar), and indicated some current, academic, liturgical thinking on mystagogy. The extent to which its 23 papers confirmed the main lines of the conclusions of my research was gratifying. Admittedly my thesis is that the Christian tradition of mystagogy is there to be used pastorally, so that the details of patristic mystagogy and of mystagogy in the different liturgical traditions are not its central issue.

The riches and limitations of the missionary lifestyle necessarily leave their mark on the work here introduced. Access to libraries is severely limited and to hope to produce a monograph deeply researched in all its details would be unrealistic. What is lacking in contact with books finds some compensation in a spread of experience, extending over several decades and many areas of pastoral endeavour, in a local Church which has been notably creative during the last quarter-century.

The light of this multiple pastoral experience, its spectrum of colours analysed through a minimal academic prism, showed me the relevance of mystagogy for today. Familiarity with the different surfaces of pastoral commitment, each with its own particular texture, showed me that the light of mystagogy was not the dull gleam of a museum-piece. Mystagogy is not just a piece of cultural history – one of those 'Storied windows, richly dight, casting a dim, religious light' – it shines on the clear air as a rainbow with potential and promise.

NOTES

1 The age-old need for initiation to adulthood and the peculiar problems this presents today are richly illustrated by Robert Bly in *Iron John: A Book About Men* (New York: Random House, 1992).

2 E. Mazza, *Mystagogy* (New York: Pueblo, 1989), is, as its subtitle reveals, a treatment of 'A Theology of Liturgy in the Patristic Age'. It is a step in the right

direction in being a study of an aspect of mystagogy made in order the better to understand the Christian liturgy; H. M. Riley's work on *Christian Initiation* is precious, but is, as its subtitle reveals, 'A Comparative Study of the Interpretations of the Baptismal Liturgy in the Mystagogical Writings of Cyril of Jerusalem, John Chrysostom, Theodore of Mopsuestia and Ambrose of Milan' (Washington: Catholic University of America Press, 1974).

3 Most of the great Catholic dictionaries and encyclopaedias of the twentieth century have no entry under mystagogy or other members of the same semantic group: the *Dictionnaire de Spiritualité* (begun in 1937) had reached vol. 10 and 'mystère' by 1980, but, amazingly, had no entry 'mystagogie'. Similarly the *New Catholic Encyclopedia* (1967) has no entry. The German *Religion in Geschichte und Gegenwart* encyclopaedia, still in the course of publication, has an entry for mystagogy, as have specialized dictionaries and encyclopaedias such as the Marietti *Dizionario Patristico e di Antichità Cristiane* (2 vols, 1984). The period at which the reintroduction of *mystagogie* and related words took place in French liturgical circles may be discovered from an examination of the *Tables décennales* for *La Maison-Dieu*:

There is no entry in the tables for 1945–54 (*LMD* no. 40bis); 1955–64 (*LMD* no. 82); 1965–74 (*LMD* no. 120). For the first time, in the tables for 1975–84 (*LMD* no. 160) there is an index item 'Mystagogie'; there are six items indexed under this heading, taken from three issues of the periodical (140, 147, 158). Since 1984 a whole issue of *La Maison-Dieu*, no. 177 (1989, 1er trimestre), has been devoted to 'Mystagogies'; no. 185 (1991) is devoted to 'Initiation Chrétienne des Adultes'.

4 A. M. Triacca and A. Pistoia (eds), *Mystagogie: Pensée liturgique d'aujourd'hui et liturgie ancienne* (Rome: Edizioni Liturgiche, 1993).

5 The use of the language of mystagogy in spiritual theology is richly presented in E. Ancilli (ed.), *Mistagogia e Direzione Spirituale* (Rome: Pontificio Istituto di Spiritualità/Milan: Edizioni O.R., 1985).

1

THE EARLY HISTORY OF MYSTAGOGY

ETYMOLOGY

Etymologically, mystagogy is the action of conducting (*agein*, to lead) a person who has been initiated (*mystēs*). Classical Greek spoke of the function of initiating into the sacred, and classical Latin followed the Greek usage. In an extended sense, someone who introduced a friend into the sacred precincts of the Greek family could be called a mystagogue; and the word mystagogy could be used of someone being initiated into the business of tax-farming. Extension of the use of the word into the secular domain made it easier for the Church Fathers to borrow it.[1] Mystagogy has to do with initiation into the sacred. The word 'mystagogy' means leading the one initiated, into the mystery (it has a root in common with the word 'pedagogy'). The 'mystagogue' is the person who does the leading, who introduces the candidate into the divine mysteries.

Patristic preachers (bishops from the fourth century) sometimes used the expression 'mystagogue' as the equivalent of 'master', applying it to God, Israel, Christ, the Prophets, the Apostles, the Evangelists, doctors and catechists. The word 'mystagogue' has not got the intellectualist tone of *didaskalos*, nor the disciplinary note of 'pedagogue'.

At the beginning of the modern era, the word 'mystagogy' was debased, sometimes to the level of being placed alongside superstition and sorcery, as signifying a practice alien to true religion. Immanuel Kant had a poor opinion of 'mystagogy', as of mysticism in general, and his attitude seems to have so frightened some contemporary theologians that they avoid the word even where it should obviously be used. These theologians are beginning to become 'modern' now, when others, having discovered the shortcomings of an exclusively rational approach to life, have left the modern age behind. The standard 'Enlightenment' theory of history saw humanity as progressing from more primitive stages, such as the mystical, to a higher one represented by themselves and their rational approach to religion. They kept their end up by playing down as obscurantist everything which they considered to belong to the medieval world, mysticism and mystagogy included.

MYSTAGOGY IN PAGAN ANTIQUITY

The mystery religions which gave birth to the expression 'mystagogy' belonged to the world of Greco-Roman antiquity and had their greatest expansion during the first three centuries AD, though their roots go much further back. The mystery religions were agricultural in origin, arising from seasonal cults to ensure fertility for crops. Many involved gods and goddesses of fertility and were first celebrated locally, but became cosmopolitan and more sophisticated with the passage of time. The 'mysteries' were secret cults into which a candidate had to be initiated – almost like secret societies. The constitutive features of a mystery society were common meals, common dances and ceremonies.

At Eleusis, near Athens, candidates were initiated especially into the Eleusinian mysteries or cult of the corn goddess Demeter or Ceres, mythological successor to Gaia, and in many Greek cities into the Dionysian mysteries. The mysteries were secret cults which allowed people to experience religion in a way not provided for in the official public religions. There were also mystery religions in Crete, Syria, and Egypt. The remote origins of the mystery cults of Syria go back to the third millennium BC, to the Sumero-Babylonian cult of Ishtar. At Rome and throughout the Empire, the Persian cult of Mithra became widespread from the second to the fourth centuries AD. The cult was probably brought from the East by soldiers and it remained a male and military mystery religion.[2]

The mystery cults were secret for several reasons, firstly because they flourished alongside the official religion, constituting an alternative religious experience; then, they may have had teachings considered subversive of the commonly received ideas about the universe; and, finally, they involved an experience and not a doctrine and so had little to tell to someone who had not undergone the experience. The Greek root of the word 'mystery' implies that those present ought to close their mouths about what they had heard or experienced; this is one of the factors making for scarcity of information about the cults.

Many participants took part in the rites of the mystery society for the sake of good fellowship, eating and drinking and (in the case of the Dionysian cults) sexual pleasure. There was, however, a deeper level of the cult, which was not expressed in words, but transmitted by the rites themselves to those who were capable of appreciating it. There was no formal theology, at least in early times, but it was the religious experience which made the initiation memorable and gave the cults their grip. While it was the seasonal death and birth of nature which suggested the mythological underpinning for the early cults, this mythology gradually became more sophisticated and at times even included the promise and hope of a better life after death.

With Plato, a change in the use of the language of mysteries is introduced. The language of mystery and the term *mystērion* begin to be used for philosophy. The ultimate aim – union with the divinity – has not changed; what has changed is the way. Mystery is now the asceticism of philosophical knowledge, leading to contemplation of the real, of beauty, the way to the divine. Plato expressed his philosophy with the help of borrowings from the ideas and vocabulary of the mystery religions; these religions, in turn, later used the imagery of Plato's dialogues to help express their myths. The word 'theology' came from these exchanges. The importance of the use made by Plato of the mysteries lies in the fact that *mystērion* was now applied, not only to the rites themselves – something in the realm of experience – but also to esoteric doctrines – something abstractly intellectual. A philosophical 'mystagogy' resulted from this.

For our knowledge of the pagan mystery religions we are indebted almost exclusively to early Christian writers. These had usually got one of two aims in referring to these rites and cults: they wanted to show how debauched they were and consequently how inferior to Christianity (much as missionaries in more recent times rarely saw anything positive in the initiation rites of African and Asiatic traditional religions), or they wanted to show those rites as diabolic counterfeits of Christian liturgy. In neither case is the quality of the witness reassuring. Information coming only from prejudiced sources makes it difficult to do justice to these religions. The Eleusinian cults were banned by the Christian Emperor Theodosius in the year 392.

Initiation into the mystery religions which, for centuries, formed part of Greek and Roman culture gave us the word 'mystagogy', but the practice of initiating candidates into an experience of the divine was not limited to those cultures. Virtually every traditional (oral) culture has, or had in the past, rites for the initiation of boys and girls into adult living. The religion of the relevant culture is integral to these rites which mark the transition from the dependent and natural state of the child to the spiritual and responsible condition of an adult. Elders accompany and guide this initiation, its rites and challenges, and are thus mystagogues, even though their languages may not have a technical expression for the role of leading the candidates into what is an eminently religious experience. The fact of a real initiation into the spirituality of adulthood has been a fundamental element in human society down the ages, with some mystagogic role of accompanying the candidates almost entirely inseparable from the practice. This initiation was prior to and underlying the specifically Christian practice of mystagogy and continued in traditional cultures during the centuries when the Church forgot about mystagogy and real initiation. This anthropological fact makes the case for its (re-)introduction valid even if mystagogy had never before existed in a specifically Christian context: some formal social preparation for the step into adult living has belonged to humanity at all times. Whether in a narrowly 'religious' field, or in a more holistically human guise, an experiential introduction of young men and women into the world of their elders would not be before its time.

MYSTAGOGY IN PATRISTIC TIMES

With the conversion of Constantine, Christianity was firmly established, and gradually from a proscribed sect became the official imperial religion (by edict of Theodosius in 380). It was too easy for those who courted the imperial favour to become Christians. A large intake of new members required some sifting process and formal ritual of entry – during the centuries of persecution conversions to Christianity for unworthy motives were, understandably, rare. The language and experiential approach of initiation for these adult converts were borrowed from the mystery religions, which had long experience with their own candidates. The fact, mentioned above, that the vocabulary of mystagogy was also sometimes used in a secular sense encouraged the Christian Fathers to borrow it – it was not inseparably bound to the pagan cults. That borrowing, with all the purifying and profound recasting which it involved, is an early and excellent example of inculturation – of the Christian faith putting down roots in the local culture through a process of give and take. Recent scholarship has made it clear that borrowing from the mystery cults did not go beyond language and external forms; more substantial roots of the Christian practice of initiation can be traced back to Judaism rather than to the traditional cults of Greece, Rome and further East.

Christian mystagogy is known to us chiefly through the homilies preached by bishops (Fathers of the Church), Cyril of Jerusalem, Ambrose, John Chrysostom, and others, who explained to the newly baptized the experience undergone during the preparation for and Easter celebration of baptism, chrism and Eucharist. Lent and Easter Week was the usual time for the mystagogic homilies.

Centuries before Christian use of the word mystagogy, the First Epistle of Peter has a largely mystagogic outlook. It builds on the experience of baptism into Christ's death and resurrection, an experience considered as recent, and tries to help those who have come from afar to feel at home in the Christian community.

A commanding notion, running through all the patristic treatment of Christian initiation, is the mystagogic note:

> Faith makes us enter into a *Mystery*, in the Pauline sense of the word, into a design of love which God has conceived from the beginning, and which is being worked out over the centuries. It is impossible to overestimate this aspect of initiation in the Fathers. It may be said that everything else comes from this and that, thanks to this, everything else becomes clear . . .
>
> The first characteristic of initiation is then, to be initiation into a mystery of love . . . infinite love was fundamental in Christian thought from the origins of the community.[3]

The pilgrim Egeria, visiting Jerusalem towards the end of the fourth century, described the Easter week mystagogic homilies addressed by the bishop to the newly baptized; she noted the need for interpretation, because of the two languages used, Greek and Syriac, and was impressed by the vigorous vocal participation of the neophytes.

For Bishop Cyril of Jerusalem (d. 386), five mystagogic homilies from Easter Week (*c*. AD 350) are preserved and are thought to merit his name, although they just could be the work of his successor John.[4] In the first of the homilies, reference is made to the later homilies simply as 'mystagogies':

> These rites were carried out in the forecourt. God willing, when we enter the holy of holies at the next stage of our mystagogies (initiation into the mysteries), we shall then become aware of the symbolism of what was there performed. (1.11)[5]

The sermons of St Cyril have often been considered the archetype of mystagogical homilies, though more recently they are seen to be only one approach to mystagogy, among several others.[6] Amongst the earliest of the genre, they are also directly related to the rites – gestures and Scripture texts – which the newly baptized have experienced in the sacraments, and comment on these rites with abundance of biblical references and typology. Cyril presents Christianity not as a doctrine or an obligation, but as a history into which the Christian must enter, and a life which the Christian must live. The first two mystagogical homilies deal with baptism, the third with confirmation and the last two with the Eucharist, doctrine and liturgy. In the first homily, Cyril gives the recently baptized a guided tour of the new demesne to which they have been given entry. They have been led out of slavery to Satan, by Jesus; his blood turning away the exterminator, as the Israelites were led out of slavery to Pharaoh by Moses, the wrath of the avenging angel having been turned away by the blood of the lamb sprinkled on the doorposts (Exod 12). The new Christians were pursued by Satan until immersed in the baptismal waters, as the Israelites were pursued by Pharaoh right up to the waves of the Red Sea. Here the typological style of patristic exegesis is clearly at work: that is, a scriptural explanation which sees the important persons, events and objects of the New Testament foreshadowed by other people, events or objects in the Old Testament – the baptized, immersed in the water of baptism, are saved from the fierce enemy as the Israelites were saved from Pharaoh by the waters of the Red Sea.

The use of typology – very widespread during the first centuries of Christian theology – was an attempt to respect the unity of Scripture as the Word of God, Old Testament as well as New. It also dealt with the problem of each biblical text having two authors, being at once the work of a human author and word of God. Behind the writer's words and intended meaning were seen deeper reaches of meaning intended by the Holy Spirit, who writes, not just with words, but with historical events. The New Testament itself gives many examples of the use of typology: Jesus is the new Adam; Moses was a prophetic figure and lawgiver, like Jesus; the sacrifice of his firstborn son, Isaac, by the patriarch Abraham was more than a hint of what God the Father would do in sacrificing his Son, Jesus; Jonah in the whale's belly for three days is like the Son of Man who spent three days in the tomb . . .

From Ambrose of Milan (d. 397) we have two sets of instructions to the recently baptized – the *De Sacramentis*, which is a compilation made up from notes taken during the preaching of the Bishop (probably about the year 391); the second – the *De Mysteriis* – is a series of homilies carefully corrected by Ambrose and revised for publication. In his homilies, which are mystagogic, without using the word (which never came to have much acceptance in Latin), Ambrose draws lessons from the rites of baptism, showing how behind the visible and tangible rites deeper and invisible effects are operative. This explanation of the rites is made from Ambrose's theology of the sacraments but, because his homilies lead the newly baptized to appreciate the Mystery of Christ in which he shows them to have participated, it is also, and by the same process, mystagogic. Going from the visible element or gesture, to the invisible reality of Christ, Ambrose is at the same time sacramental and mystagogic. For him the *mystery* was this invisible reality of

Christ, underlying the sacramental material and rite, and the Greek word *mystērion*, for mystery, was soon replaced by the Latin word *sacramentum* which gave us the word 'sacrament'.[7] It is this sort of theology of the liturgy which led Enrico Mazza to claim that mystagogy is just that, a patristic theology of the liturgy.[8]

Ambrose develops the theology of baptism:

> You came into the baptistry, you saw the water, you saw the bishop, you saw the levite . . . You saw all you could see with the eyes of the body, all that is open to human sight. You saw what is seen, but not what is done. What is unseen is much greater than what is seen . . .[9]

> You saw the water, but not all waters have a curative power: only that water has it which has the grace of Christ. There is a difference between the matter and its consecration, between the action and its effect. The action belongs to the water, its effect to the Holy Spirit.[10]

Again, and also in reference to water and to the effect of baptism:

> You went there, you washed, you came to the altar, you began to see what you had not seen before: that is to say, through the font of the Lord and the preaching of the Lord's passion your eyes were opened. Before you seemed to be blind of heart; but now you began to perceive the light of the sacraments (*coepisti lumen sacramentorum videre*).[11]

These passages, and especially the last one, illustrate Ambrose's notion of mystagogy as bound up with the effect of the sacrament itself, as is the case with Chrysostom too. They also show the conviction that the eyes of the soul being opened was fundamental to initiation, and this seems to have been due both to the preaching and to the 'washing'. The reference to Christ's miracle of curing the man born blind (John 9) is evident.

In general 'Ambrose can attribute the same meaning to more than one rite' and he:

> can assign various meanings to the same ritual action, . . . while a scholastic would distinguish between different kinds of causality, as a mystagogue Ambrose does not make such distinctions: he simply says different things in different contexts . . . Thus, due to the pastoral nature of mystagogy, the meaning Ambrose gives to an individual rite seems to depend more on the particular theological point he finds it necessary to make at a given moment, or on the specific Scriptural text which comes to him on a given occasion to make that point, than on a pre-established one-to-one correspondence between rite and theological meaning.[12]

The poetic style of Scripture – psalms, parables and hymns – is still present in a spirituality which has not yet become philosophically limiting and theologically prosaic.

John Chrysostom (d. 407) uses expressions referring to initiation more frequently than do other Fathers who speak of mystagogy. This is partly due to the volume of his writings which have reached us. The baptismal rite itself he thought of as the initiation and this he calls mystagogy, a name he does not give to anything before or after the sacramental celebration. Baptism and Eucharist then become the mystagogy *par excellence*. This cultic use of the language of mystagogy is a development which goes beyond its use to designate words of explanation of the liturgy pronounced after the sacramental celebration,[13] so that, in Chrysostom's use, the expression 'mystagogy' usually means the rites of initiation, as they existed in his day, taken as a whole – renouncing the devil, baptism and Eucharist. It is consistent with this that Chrysostom's baptismal homilies were preached before Easter Night. It is the initiation which opens the eyes of faith, brings into the sanctuary, or associates the neophyte with the song of the angels. The sacraments themselves may be seen as prime factors in this illumination – as themselves the supreme *words*, speaking more loudly than any homily. Initiation would then become initiation into the truths of faith, *through* the sacraments and not initiation *to* the sacraments. Any catechesis on the occasion of the initiation only serves to enhance this role of the sacraments as themselves *the* mystagogy. It is based on this view of mystagogy that some contemporary theologians think it a matter of indifference to use the language of the catechumenate for the Christian formation of those baptized in infancy, but no longer practising.

Chrysostom's baptismal homilies are not commentaries on the liturgical rites of initiation as were those of Cyril of Jerusalem; they aim rather at arousing emotion and moral sense. Rather than expounding the Mystery in itself, they draw moral teaching about the Christian life from it. They were preached to the whole community and not just to the neophytes. To Chrysostom we owe insistence on the awesome character of the Christian mysteries – their capacity for making the recipients' hair stand on end:[14]

> Chrysostom, in the mêlée of the secular empire and the Church's struggle to maintain her unique identity vis-à-vis the 'embarrassing' peace with this empire, shows his candidates how the life, cross and death of Jesus, which once took place in the past, reveal themselves again in the encounter of the Christian with the radical challenges which the secular city provides.[15]

This historical factor accounts for the moral tone of the homilies. Speaking of the exorcisms, for which the candidates took off their outer garments and stood on sack-cloth, he says:

The wonderful, unbelievable thing is that every difference and distinction of rank is missing here. If anyone happens to be in a position of worldly importance of conspicuous wealth, if he boasts of his birth or the glory of this present life, he stands on just the same footing as the beggar in rags, the blind man or the lame. Nor does he complain at this since he knows that all such differences have been set aside in the life of the spirit; a grateful heart is the only requirement.[16]

Theodore of Mopsuestia (d. 428), friend and fellow student of Chrysostom, was ordained at Antioch about 383 and became bishop of Mopsuestia, in Cilicia, about a hundred miles from Antioch, in 392. Because the Greek text of his homilies is not extant, it is not easy to trace a mystagogical vocabulary in his preaching. Many of his works are now missing, because he was condemned by the Fifth General Council (Constantinople, in 553), over a century after his death, for preparing the way for Nestorianism, and his writings were destroyed. His orthodoxy is now defended. For him, the liturgical signs bring about the present reality of the past salvific events of Christ's death and resurrection, and the future hope hidden in those symbols is guaranteed by the resurrection of Christ; he sees the baptismal birth and resurrection as symbol of the real beginning of the future realization of what is now contained in promise.[17]

Theodore, too, like Ambrose, is capable of giving quite different interpretations to the same ritual element. In the opening sentences of his first homily on the Eucharist – considered mystagogic – Theodore says that the deacons' stole (*orarion*), worn on the left shoulder and hanging down both in front and behind, makes one think of Christ being led to his passion. Further on in the same homily he says that the deacons are vested in clothes adapted to the splendour of their ministry; and he again comments on the same rubric which says that the diaconal stole 'rests on the left shoulder and hangs down at both sides', in front and behind. This, Theodore says, is the sign that the deacons do not exercise a servile ministry but a free one; the realities to which they minister lead those who belong to the household of God – the Church – to freedom.

In the same homily two quite different interpretations are given to the one ritual element. Theodore apparently was not embarrassed by this fact. The explanation would seem to be that same one given by Pamela Jackson and quoted above, in relation to Ambrose's mystagogy, namely that for the pastoral significance of symbols, there is no one-to-one correspondence between ritual element and theological explanation.

It was Theodore who introduced this allegorical practice of comparing ritual elements of the eucharistic celebration with events of Christ's passion, interpreting the Eucharist as a ritual allegory that re-enacts the events of

Jesus' passion, death, burial and resurrection. This sort of allegorizing opened the way for the medieval practice of commenting on the liturgy in terms, not of itself, for its origins and symbolism had become obscure, but of extrinsic and often fantastic connections.[18] Recognizing that the Mass was somehow a re-enactment of Christ's passion, the medieval allegorizers, in their sermons and explanations, attached to each visible or audible element in the rite an extrinsic interpretation drawn from the passion story.

Allegorizing, with the exaggerations that contributed to the reaction of the Reformation, was a by-product of the use of Greek philosophy in reflections on Scripture. It was one of the first steps on the downward path which led to the abandoning of the historical understanding of the Bible and to its transformation into a source-book for timeless theological norms and doctrines. The Bible is an account of God's interventions in human history on behalf of his people. The two Testaments are not simply linked by theological and invisible bonds, but there is a real historical continuity between them. Paul's eschatology saw the new era – the end time of God's Kingdom – as not only announced, but inaugurated by the coming of Jesus Christ. He saw history as stretching towards the Second Coming and the fullness of the Kingdom. The newly emerging theology, based on Greek philosophical thinking, removed the historical dimension and turned Christianity into a new 'religion' – 'the only true and universal religion of humankind'.[19] The tension between this present age and the one to come was changed into a vertical opposition between time and eternity.

Allegorical thinking, instead of seeing the Old Testament as historical preparation for the New, saw it as a shadowy promise which found fulfilment in Jesus. This change in the role of Jesus Christ, from ratifier of God's on-going action in history to one of fulfilment of the promises, left no room for the Second Coming. This distortion of salvation history is with us still: it abolishes the final and future Christ event of salvation history and reduces the future, for the Christian, to an individual dying – 'my eternal salvation', rather than the joyful Coming of Christ.

Maximus the Confessor (d. 662) became a monk after a career in public administration at Constantinople (First Secretary to the Emperor Heraclius) and suffered exile, imprisonment and mutilation (having his tongue and hand cut off) in his struggles against the Monothelite heretics (who held that there was only one will in Christ). More theologian and mystic than pastor, he is concerned, like Chrysostom, to draw spiritual lessons on the occasion of the liturgical rites rather than to give a commentary on the rites themselves. He wrote a *Mystagogia*. Elements of Greek philosophy, especially Aristotelian, and Christian theology, especially that of Pseudo-Dionysius, are fused into a synthesis which leads some to consider him the Father of Byzantine theology. Maximus sees the human as an image of the cosmos and the human and divine as finding their synthesis in Christ. In Maximus's day this christological synthesis was possible; it would not have been possible earlier, before the christological truths had become established; later was too late – other challenges had stolen attention.

At the time when he most likely wrote his *Mystagogia*, many were leaving the Church in disillusionment and his purpose in writing seems to have been to recall them to their earlier faith (a few years later the first Islamic incursions would lead to the reaction of greater Christian solidarity).[20] Maximus gave a new twist to mystagogy, taking it away from the people – where it had, in any case, almost died out – and making it monastic. The trend accompanied the shift of emphasis in Church life, from the city to the desert, which came about after the end of the persecutions. To be simply Christian was no longer something heroic – everybody wanted to join, since it had become the imperial 'thing to do' – and to be an authentic follower of Christ seemed to call for something more, something special.

Various movements arose, some of them suspect, which endeavoured to perpetuate the heroic path. Important among these was the movement out of the cities, where imperial administrative posts, honours and luxury had their seat, and into the desert – the place where Israel had become hardened for conquest of the Promised Land and where Christ had done combat with Satan.

In its patristic centuries, then, mystagogy was already seen as a pastoral practice for the recuperation of those of the baptized who had grown disillusioned and indifferent – towards the Church if not towards Christ.

Some are of the opinion that Maximus summed up and enriched all the preceding tradition of mystagogy.[21] For Maximus mystagogy consists in helping the Christian to gain knowledge (*gnōsis*) of the Mystery through contemplating it with the spiritual senses which function as a seeing and hearing which, however, have no visible or audible object. This spiritual sensing can only be accomplished through seeking the Mystery where it is to be found: in creation; in Scripture; in the liturgy, as mediated by symbols. Mystagogy is the means by which this is done. His *Mystagogia* includes a commentary on the Byzantine Liturgy, of which this is a small sample; it shows Maximus's allegorizing tendency:

> The closing of the doors of the holy church of God after the reverent reading of the holy Gospel and the catechumens' dismissal, expresses first the passing away of material things; then the future entrance of the worthy into the spiritual world (or bridal chamber of Christ) after that dread banishment and even more formidable final reckoning; and lastly the total repudiation of the illusions in the senses.[22]

For patristic theology in general, faith makes us enter into a mystery, in St

Paul's sense of the word, into a design of love which God has conceived from the beginning, and which is being worked out over the centuries. The first characteristic of initiation is that it introduces into a mystery of God's love in Christ. The second characteristic is that this initiation is always, at the same time, initiation into a community. Patristic mystagogy applied to both aspects – mystery and community – of this initiation process as a whole. Similarly, the neophyte had at one and the same time a religious experience of the Mystery of Christ and of insertion into the Christian community. Only when each of these fundamental experiences of Christian faith was re-emphasized with Vatican II could the revival of mystagogy make sense once more.

It was in Alexandria that the great school for catechists was set up and made famous by men such as Clement of Alexandria and Origen. These teachers took on the pagan thinkers on their own ground of philosophy. They used the language of the mysteries in an abstract, philosophical sense, presenting Christianity as the one true philosophy, rather in the manner of Plato.

The Fathers, especially the Greek ones, employed the language of mystagogy with an increasing sureness of touch and exemplified inculturation in a rich way. Christian liturgy gradually created the setting in which mystagogy found its place. The liturgical structures set up for the initiation of adult converts to Christianity were often participated in by the rest of the Church community as a spiritual experience of renewal of faith. The classical edifice of Christian initiation as a whole has bequeathed to us the liturgical season of Lent, whereby the spirit of their initiation could be recaptured by all the baptized. Something of the liturgical structure has carried over from the golden age of the catechumenate (from the fourth to the seventh centuries), albeit in a fragmented form which lacks the unified vision of faith characteristic of the early centuries; but nothing of the mystagogic element survived.

When the Church was living its period of initial growth, the catechumenate was the distinctive feature of its life and shaped its liturgy, theology and spirituality. Of the initiatory stages: evangelization, catechumenate and sacramental celebration on Easter Night, mystagogy alone was left when the stream of candidates for adult baptism dried up. Mystagogy was then, or should have been, a spirituality of growth and deepening for the whole Christian community. Formerly (at least in places), all had shared in the mystagogy with the neophytes; when the situation of Christendom changed and there were virtually no more candidates for adult baptism, mystagogy should have been the tonic of the whole Church – an annual reliving and deepening of the initiatory experience, in the Spirit – and in places perhaps it was – in the observances of Lent. Too soon, however, it became the concern of monks alone; later, even they lost sight of the ancient tradition and mystagogy simply faded and disappeared, at least in the Western Church.

As already mentioned, a factor which contributed to the shelving of mystagogy was the abuse of allegory in the interpretation of the biblical and liturgical elements of the rites of initiation. The Fathers used typology especially to explain the link between the Old and New Testaments, seeing aspects of the Christ event as prefigured in Old Testament personages and happenings. Wishing to get back beyond merely superficial resemblances they used a 'spiritual' type of exegesis which, however, sometimes departed too far from the literal sense of Scripture and became downright arbitrary. Interpretation of liturgical symbolism, begun by the Fathers, tended to become more and more removed from the original sense the rites had when they were first introduced. In medieval times extravagant use of allegory was often due to ignorance of the historical origins of the rites.

Reaction against medieval exaggeration in the use of allegory contributed to the Reformers' fierce insistence on the literal sense of biblical texts. This exclusive insistence on literal exegesis seems to have made it difficult for the Churches which issued from the Reformation to recover the ancient tradition of mystagogy; not having an authoritative arbiter of doctrine, they were too afraid of wild allegorizing to take to mystagogy[23] – nor were they as given to citing the Fathers as were Catholics. Mystagogy, while it does not demand details of allegorical interpretation of Scripture, does call for a broad vision of biblical theology which goes beyond any one text or set of texts; in our times it calls for a broad hermeneutic – amounting to a *sensus plenior* – based on a pastorally inspired reading of the Bible.

There are no signs of a recovery of mystagogy in the Churches which issued from the Protestant Reformation. This judgement necessarily results rather from the absence of visible evidence than from an exhaustive search of the literature of so many Churches and denominations. Reacting against the abuse of allegorizing in medieval times, the Reformers were determined not to deviate from the literal sense of biblical texts. Literal/verbal exegesis grew up in lands of Protestant culture. Most Churches which issued from the Reformation, even in recent times, are wary of allegorizing.[24]

The Anglican Communion, most likely of the Protestant Churches to recover venerable patristic notions, because of its strong sacramental theology, has carried out research on the history of Christian initiation as a whole[25] and on the specific pastoral theme of adult initiation.[26] Return to some of the abandoned patristic methods of interpretation, and a new appreciation of the *sensus plenior*, may yet allow of the rediscovery of mystagogy in the Churches issued from the Reformation.[27] It has recently been argued that in recognizing their own early tradition – dating back, notably to Lancelot Andrewes – Anglicans could recapture a mystagogic strain.[28]

Mystagogy is seen to have a long and respectable history. It dates from pre-

Christian times when it originated with a religious meaning. The elements of religious experience: seeing, feeling, hearing, as well as the less tangible experience of the Spirit, are inseparable from mystagogy. Only when religious experience is once more in honour theologically has there been any possibility of reviving interest in the practice of mystagogy. Mystagogy is also meaningless apart from the sense of a unified vision of the mystery of God's intervention in human history, and could not survive the splintering brought about by later intellectualizing developments in theology and catechetics. The demise of mystagogy was due, not only to the move to an intellectual theology, but also to the atomizing of the view of faith consequent on this. Only when each aspect of Christian tradition was recovered – respect for religious experience as of theological value and a unified view of faith centred on the Mystery of Christ – could mystagogy reappear as a realistic pastoral practice.

NOTES

1   P. De Roten, 'Le vocabulaire mystagogique de Saint Jean Chrysostome' in A. M. Triacca and A. Pistoia (eds), *Mystagogie: Pensée liturgique d'aujourd'hui et liturgie ancienne* (Rome: Edizioni Liturgiche, 1993), p. 116, quoting Liddell and Scott's *Greek–English Lexicon*.

2   Readable accounts of the mysteries and their underlying myths are to be found in Joseph Campbell, *The Masks of God*, vols 3: *Occidental Mythology* (Harmondsworth: Penguin, 1976/New York: Arkana, 1991) and 4: *Creative Mythology* (Harmondsworth: Penguin, 1982/New York: Arkana, 1991).

3   J. Lecuyer, 'Théologie de l'Initiation chrétienne d'après les Pères', *LMD* 58 (1959), p. 6. This statement by a renowned patristic scholar is important, lest the fragmentary treatment of the Fathers, necessitated by the limits of this study, result in a loss of unified vision. Although not employing the expression 'mystagogy' (the International Montserrat meeting on Pastoral Liturgy, at which his paper was read, was held in 1958, before the recovery of the expression), Lecuyer gives a clear description of the substance of the notion.

4   In order to leave the question open, recent scholars call these homilies simply 'The Jerusalem Mystagogies'; for example, P.-M. Gy, 'La mystagogie dans la liturgie ancienne et dans la pensée liturgique d'aujourd'hui' in A. M. Triacca and A. Pistoia (eds), *Mystagogie*, pp. 137–44.

5   E. Yarnold, *The Awe-Inspiring Rites of Initiation* (Slough: St Paul, 1972), p. 73. I have replaced the word 'mystagogies', which was in parentheses, by Yarnold's paraphrase, which was not. (There is now a new edition of Fr Yarnold's valuable work: Collegeville, MN: Liturgical Press/Edinburgh: T. & T. Clark, 1994.)

6   Cf. P.-M. Gy, 'La mystagogie dans la liturgie ancienne', p. 143.

7   E. Mazza, *Mystagogy: A Theology of Liturgy in the Patristic Age* (New York: Pueblo, 1989), pp. 30f., underlines this mystagogic theology, which becomes the theme of his book.

8 E. Mazza, *Mystagogy*. Mazza agrees with Daniélou that the application of typology to Scripture is spiritual exegesis while its application to liturgy is mystagogy (p. 9).

9 *De Sacr.* I, 10; E. Yarnold, *The Awe-Inspiring Rites of Initiation*, p. 103.

10 *De Sacr.* I, 15; E. Yarnold, op. cit., p. 105.

11 *De Sacr.* III, 15; E. Yarnold, op. cit., p. 127.

12 P. Jackson, 'The meaning of *Spiritale Signaculum* in the mystagogy of Ambrose of Milan', *Ecclesia Orans* 7 (1990/91), pp. 82–3.

13 P.-M. Gy, 'La notion chrétienne d'initiation', *LMD* 132 (1977), p. 37; this article has been updated, at Gy's suggestion, by P. De Roten, 'Le vocabulaire mystagogique de Saint Jean Chrysostome' in A. M. Triacca and A. Pistoia (eds), *Mystagogie*, pp. 115–36, which is largely followed throughout this section on Chrysostom.

14 E. Yarnold, *The Awe-Inspiring Rites of Initiation*, p. 56. Yarnold takes the title of his book from Chrysostom and others who use this sort of language: ibid., p. ix.

15 H. M. Riley, *Christian Initiation: A Comparative Study of the Interpretations of the Baptismal Liturgy in the Mystagogical Writings of Cyril of Jerusalem, John Chrysostom, Theodore of Mopsuestia and Ambrose of Milan* (Washington: Catholic University of America Press, 1974), p. 453.

16 *Baptismal Homily* 2, 13; E. Yarnold, *The Awe-Inspiring Rites of Initiation*, p. 163.

17 H. M. Riley, *Christian Initiation*, p. 454; E. Yarnold, op. cit., p. 174.

18 Cf. N. Mitchell, *Cult and Controversy: The Worship of the Eucharist Outside Mass* (New York: Pueblo, 1990), pp. 49f. As regards the allegorical interpretation of liturgy, so beloved of Amalar of Metz, Righetti – severe on the genre – says that: 'By *liturgical mysticism* I understand a symbolic or allegorical interpretation, extraneous to its institution and arbitrarily attributed to an object or rite with a view to the edification of the faithful': M. Righetti, *Storia Liturgica* (Milan: Ancora, 1950), 1, p. 46. Cf. also J. A. Jungmann, *The Mass of the Roman Rite: Its Origins and Development (Missarum Sollemnia)* trans. from the German (New York: Benziger, 1951), 1, p. 87.

19 Cf. D. Bosch, *Transforming Mission* (Maryknoll, NY: Orbis, 1991), pp. 196–7, for an illuminating analysis of this process.

20 Cf. J. Stead, *St Maximus the Confessor* (Still River, MA: St Bede's Publications, 1982), p. 7.

21 M. A. Schreiber, 'Mistagogia: comunicazione e vita spirituale', *Ephemerides Carmeliticae* 28 (1977), p. 29.

22 St Maximus the Confessor, *Mystagogia*, ch. 15: J. Stead, *St Maximus the Confessor*, pp. 92–3.

23 The *Enciclopedia Garzanti di Filosofia* (1991), discussing 'allegoria', in scriptural exegesis, is of the opinion that the use of allegory requires a controlling authority to fix the rules: 'Se non c'è più l'autorità della chiesa a fissare i codici dell'interpretazione allegorica, tale interpretazione va abbandonata' (p. 17).

24 For an example, see: W. S. Lasor, 'The *Sensus Plenior* and biblical interpretation' in Donald K. McKim (ed.), *A Guide to Contemporary Hermeneutics* (Grand Rapids: Eerdmans, 1986), p. 55. On reading the above text, Dr P. Leonard points out that the great seventeenth-century Puritan work of devotion, John Bunyan's *Pilgrim's Progress*, is an allegory. This anomaly is explained in the *New Catholic Encyclopedia* article on Bunyan by M. Williams, who says that Bunyan's rich religious allegory is written in terms of his own life, rather than the Bible,

and seems to owe much to the pre-Reformation morality plays and to popular preaching.

25 J. D. C. Fischer, *Christian Initiation: Baptism in the Medieval World. A Study of the Disintegration of the Primitive Rite of Initiation* (London: SPCK, Alcuin Club Collection 47, 1965); and *Christian Initiation, the Reformation Period* (London: SPCK, Alcuin Club 51, 1970).

26 D. A. Withey (ed.), *Adult Initiation* (Papers delivered at the Conference of the Society for Liturgical Study 1988; Nottingham: Grove Books, 1989). If, on the one hand, the Roman Catholic recovery of the RCIA is admired, the only reference to the term 'mystagogy' in the series of essays is contained in the description of the stages of the Catholic RCIA. Ironically, the mention is made by an Anglican author and not by the Roman Catholic contributor.

27 Cf. W. S. Lasor, 'The *Sensus Plenior*', pp. 47–64.

28 N. Lossky, 'Y a-t-il une mystagogie anglicane?' in A. M. Triacca and A. Pistoia (eds), *Mystagogie*, pp. 189–99.

2

THE RECOVERY OF MYSTAGOGY

At the time of Vatican II, a number of factors contributed to make some rediscovery of mystagogy possible. The fundamentally pastoral character given the Council by Pope John XXIII opened the way for a unified vision of Christian faith that would go beyond the refining of concepts into which theology had sunk. The great renewal movements in biblical studies, patrology and liturgy, at work since the last century, contributed a base of serious study to the pastoral impulse. Irrelevance, not heresy, was the danger threatening the Church and was clearly identified by the Pope. Concern for contemporary men and women, whose culture was little catered for by the theology in vogue, was a pastoral preoccupation.

An esoteric language, reserved to a privileged caste of clerics, had rarely addressed the great problems of the age. A laity, some of whom were highly educated, required access to the deepest fonts of Christian life and were poorly catered for by the arid theology and devotional pabulum currently on offer. Above all, theology and catechesis had become excessively intellectual and ignored the element of experience that contemporary culture was rediscovering and that is fundamental in mystagogy. The ill-directed attempts of the Modernists to bring back experience to theology had provoked a reaction that reinforced the divide between theory and practice, grace and nature, and left the argument from authority paramount in theology.[1] But newer efforts had been made and by the 1960s the time was ripe for a more balanced and biblical theology, allowing history, experience and the action of the Spirit a greater place once more.

To have reinstated the Bible was a victory for Vatican II. God is revealed in the history of the People of Israel and the history of this people is the starting-point for theology; these emphases each allow a role to human experience. The Council's recognition that the needs of our time are relevant to liturgical celebration opened doors to celebrating aspects of the human experience of the Christian community. The singling out of the Paschal Mystery of Christ as the high point of liturgy (because it is the centre of our salvation as known in biblical relevation) proved fundamental to any possibility of real initiation. Besides being objectively central, the Mystery, which is historical, has enormous psychological potential. To have identified that centre – centre also of patristic preaching – gave religious education a new impulse. It is now possible – it is still more a possibility than a realization – to focus every aspect of life on the central Mystery of Christ that gives meaning to everything Christian.[2]

The theology provided by the Council was biblically based and closer to spirituality than was Scholasticism. The experience of men and women of today was the starting-point of *Gaudium et Spes* and their joys and sorrows were counted as relevant to their Christian life. Religious experience was no longer outlawed; it was even accepted, together with study and episcopal preaching, as a way in which tradition grows.[3]

Since the time of the Second Vatican Council there are chiefly three areas of pastoral interest that have adopted and regularly employ the language of mystagogy:

1. Liturgical mystagogy, closely linked to sacramental initation, now restored in the *Ordo* for the Christian Initiation of Adults.

2. The mystagogy for modern men and women living in a world in crisis of religion. This use of the language of mystagogy was introduced by Karl Rahner in 1966, and has since been taken up by others.

3. The mystagogy of mysticism or spiritual theology. The language of mystagogy is used of the spiritual direction of those who seek to experience the Mystery in mysticism.

Of these three areas, liturgical renewal, especially, received a great impulse at the Council, which ordered a revision of the baptismal rites. A real catechumenate was to be restored: 'a period of suitable instruction (*aptae institutioni destinatum*) . . . sanctified by rites to be celebrated at successive intervals of time'.[4] The rite of baptism of adults was to be revised in the light of the restoration of the catechumenate.[5] Finally, the rite of baptism of *children* was to be revised, 'taking into account the fact that those to be baptized are infants'.[6] For 1,500 years, since children had gradually come to constitute the majority of those to be baptized in the Churches of the lands once belonging to the Greco-Roman empire, a form of the adult rite of baptism had been used for infants; the same rite being used for adults. This confusion was finally to be sorted out.

Some scholars have discerned in the restoration of the Easter Vigil, in 1955, the immediate spur towards a restoration of Christian initiation specifically for adults. New emphasis on the original importance of the Vigil for Christian initiation obviously pointed in this direction, and reflection leading to the separation of the rite destined for the baptism of infants from that for adults helped towards an appreciation of the factors involved in Christian initiation. But the greatest impulse towards a revival of mystagogy came from the reintroduction of a catechumenate. The studies necessary for the drawing up of the restored catechumenate, and those for its fruitful pastoral implementation, led to research on the ancient mystagogic practice of the Church of the Fathers.

THE CHRISTIAN INITIATION OF ADULTS

In 1962 the Congregation of Rites had published an *Ordo baptismi adultorum per gradus catechumenatus dispositi*. This, though considered by some as mere archaeologizing, had helped renew the notion of a real catechumenate, and served to stimulate experiences with stages in the Christian initiation of adults. Its seven stages did not include one for mystagogy, but the controlled experiment helped prepare the way for the post-Conciliar *Ordo*.[7]

The new *Ordo* for the Christian Initiation of Adults (RCIA), giving effect to the Council's decision as to the restoration of the catechumenate, was promulgated on 6 January 1972 by the Congregation for Divine Worship. In the words of an Introduction to the US English-language version, 'For the first time since the patristic age, the Latin West possessed rites of initiation for adults that were not merely the rearrangement or evolution of baptismal rites for children'.[8] The 1972 *Ordo* follows the general outline of the catechumenate as it existed in patristic times, prescribing four distinct periods of inquiry and growth. These four periods are:

1. Evangelization: A period of inquiry on the part of the candidate and of evangelization and precatechumenate on the part of the Church. This ends with the rite of admittance into the catechumenate.

2. Catechumenate: Once admitted the catechumen begins a period of catechesis which may last several years. It closes with the rite of choice (election) to go forward to the lenten preparation.

3.   Sacramental Celebration: The intense period of the lenten liturgy with its purification and enlightenment prepares for celebration of the Easter Vigil, during which the candidates receive the sacraments of initiation: baptism, confirmation and Eucharist. The catechumenate ends in the Easter joy of new-born Christians. The three sacraments of initiation are celebrated together so as to respect the unity of the Paschal Mystery.

4.   Mystagogy: The final period, after Easter, is that of mystagogy.[9]

The Sunday Masses in Eastertime are singled out by the RCIA as especially appropriate for the mystagogy. Speaking of the 'Time of Mystagogy', the RCIA says:

> This is a time for the community and the neophytes together to grow in deepening their grasp of the paschal mystery and in making it part of their lives through meditation on the Gospel, sharing in the eucharist, and doing the works of charity . . .[10]

> The neophytes are, as the term 'mystagogy' suggests, introduced into a fuller and more effective understanding of mysteries through the Gospel message they have learned and above all through their experience of the sacraments they have received. For they have truly been renewed in mind, tasted more deeply the sweetness of God's word, received the fellowship of the Holy Spirit, and grown to know the goodness of the Lord. Out of this experience, which belongs to Christians and increases as it is lived, they derive a new perception of the faith, of the Church, and of the world.[11]

A report on the first years of use of the RCIA in parishes in the US saw 15 per cent of parishes employing the Rite. The whole parish benefited from the community-based celebration of the initiation of new members. It became clear that initiation into the Church is not a single ritual step, nor a course, but a process. In that country new regulations were issued, in 1988, to cater for situations which arose frequently and were causing confusion: the presence together of non-baptized persons; of those baptized in other Christian denominations and wishing now to become members of the Catholic Church; and of persons baptized, in the Catholic or other Church, but never adequately catechized.

Was the novelty of the revival of mystagogy not lost sight of in the excitement caused by the restoration of a real rite for a catechumenate in progressive stages? The mystagogical element in the Rite does not receive emphasis from the commentators, but is mentioned as an afterthought to the other stages. Was the widespread attempt to use the RCIA as a sort of 'post-baptismal catechumenate' for those long baptized not in part due to catechists and catechetical experts not having understood the full scope and possibilities of mystagogy? This question becomes more acute when one considers that mystagogy today is promoted by those interested in spirituality and those concerned with liturgy. Catechetical specialists have not discovered the potential of mystagogy as an answer to their problems.[12] As will appear throughout this book, mystagogy should be thought of as an aspect of all religious formation and not limited to a final stage in the process of sacramental initiation where it is little understood and only receives formal treatment. It can also become a valid pastoral instrument for the recuperation of those baptized but now grown indifferent – an instrument so used by Maximus the Confessor.

Mystagogy was exiled for 1,200 years when theology left mysticism and Christian experience behind. Now that experience, rather than obedience, is the keynote of the culture, mystagogy should find once more a hearty welcome. Why does it not? We are now, once more, in a pastoral age: making transparent the ways to life; the sources of vital energy are more relevant than calls to doctrinal obedience. The Mystery is not outside and above life, but is its hidden face, waiting to be discovered through appropriate experience. The experience into which the mystagogue led the candidate was not just any experience, but experience of the central Mystery of Christ's death and resurrection. The unifying of faith, through focusing it on what is objectively central, is another strength of mystagogy relevant to our times. The Paschal Mystery is the historical centre of Christian faith, clearly identified by Vatican II. Insistence on a unifying centre is recognized as fundamental in religious education today. Mystagogy aims at the centre and always sees other aspects of the Mystery as leading towards that. Why is it that, in spite of the fact that it was reintroduced by the *Ordo* and includes key aspects of the best contemporary religious education, mystagogy still remains, for all practical purposes, in exile? It suffices to examine the manuals of catechetics to see that catechists, enthusiastic about the RCIA, remain indifferent to mystagogy.

A sad example of the influence of long-standing custom shows how mystagogy has been subsumed under catechetics. Translators of the Latin text of the *Ordo initiationis christianae adultorum* into English, when they came to the crucial paragraph (37), translated the word 'mystagogy' as 'post-baptismal catechesis or mystagogy'.[13]

Although formally placing mystagogy as last of the four stages, the *Ordo* implies a view of mystagogy that does not limit it to a final stage, but sees it as running through the whole process of initiation.[14] When it treats of the first of the four stages (a precatechumenate), that of evangelization, the *Ordo* says:

> From evangelization, completed with the help of God, come the faith
> and initial conversion that cause a person to feel called away from sin
> and drawn into the mystery of God's love. (37)

A word like 'feeling', and reference to being 'drawn into the mystery of God's love', belong to the language of mystagogy, present even in this first stage of the initiation process. At the second stage, that of the catechumenate proper, when dealing with catechesis, the *Ordo* again uses the language of mystagogy:

> This catechesis leads the catechumens not only to an appropriate acquaintance with dogmas and precepts but also to a profound sense of the mystery of salvation in which they desire to participate. (75.1)

Aspects of the definition of mystagogy are present here – to lead the candidate into an experience of the Mystery of Christ. The *Ordo*, then, accepts in practice religious experience at all stages of the initiation and focuses on the Mystery of Christ, while limiting formal mention of mystagogy to a fourth and final stage. It could well have admitted that mystagogy is a vital aspect of the initiation as a whole, throughout every chronological stage.

The liturgy is the Church's traditional *locus* of religious experience, but liturgy today must develop considerably if it is to provide such experience and begin to exercise once more its mystagogic function. Fire, light and water, each symbolizing either life or destruction, have always been mystagogic material. Now our liturgical use of them is become banal. We must go further. The Alleluia sung in tongues; free-floating prayer; personal experience fed into the community: these elements of charismatic renewal must be incorporated once more into the liturgy, to which they once belonged, so that Sunday worship may recover its mystagogic potential for producing a living religious experience.

A symbolism which speaks to contemporary men and women must take its place alongside older ritual elements, which in turn must be situated in their biblical and historical contexts – the role of the homily is important here. Clean water, pure air, green leaves, non-toxic food – for all God's children on this planet – must be celebrated with the food and drink (bread and wine). The dynamism and concern of movements and groups that struggle for ecological balance, Third World liberation, racial, religious and sexual equality; that engage in protest marches for these causes, and for the rights of minorities and of those discriminated against, must be incorporated into liturgy as integral to a contemporary understanding of the Christian Mystery. They are the places where the Spirit is seen at work and God heard speaking most readily today. If properly understood, in the light of a theology which is adequate to its contemporary task, work at each of these concerns can be mystagogic. These preoccupations of our times are ultimately linked to aspects of the total Mystery of Christ, crucified, risen and coming in his Kingdom.

MYSTAGOGY FOR THE CHRISTIAN IN THE WORLD

It was Karl Rahner who, in the years immediately following on Vatican II, first gave currency to the revived notion of mystagogy (albeit timidly as some would have it). His thought on the matter is to be found in the *Handbuch der Pastoraltheologie*, of 1966, and in an article published in volume 7 of the *Schriften zur Theologie* (*Theological Investigations*), published in the same year. Mystagogy as a response to the pastoral challenges of a secularized world is emphasized in the *Handbuch*: personal experience of the transcendental dimension of life is a necessity if the individual is to be a Christian in that world. For this personal experience a wise and skilled guide is necessary. Rahner spells out a spirituality for contemporary men and women of the First World in the article 'Christian living formerly and today', in *Theological Investigations*. Well versed in patristic lore, and perhaps precisely because of his familiarity with the Fathers, Rahner can transpose the early Christian practice of mystagogy into a modern key to make it relevant to the pastoral needs of his country and his time.

For Rahner, the Church finds itself in deep crisis because of the rethinking required in order to attune itself to the historical situation and the needs of the hour. For him, a spirituality for tomorrow is the decisive question, 'The devout Christian of the future will either be a "mystic", one who has "experienced" something, or he will cease to be anything at all.'[15] The 'Christian living' which this spirituality involves is complex, varying according to age and sex, nationality and culture, and worldly avocations; emphasis here is on European middle-class lay people, for whom Rahner tries to find a 'mysticism for beginners.'

When Karl Rahner reintroduces mystagogy into Catholic theology and spirituality he brings it up to date for modern Christians, long baptized, and for other people – doubting, grieving, seeking. He bases his mystagogy rather on the style of the exercises of Ignatius of Loyola, with his discernment of spirits, than on the sacramental rites of initiation.[16]

For our present purposes, the importance of Rahner's revival of mystagogy lies in the courage and lucidity with which he took a patristic notion and translated it into the categories of contemporary pastoral concern. The great patristic mystagogues were very conscious of the ecclesial, political or social position and situation of their hearers; the same is true of Rahner. The global situation has changed so much since the seventh century that Rahner's project for rereading mystagogy stands out as particularly creative and prophetic.[17] Translation and rereading is a constant hermeneutic necessity so that ancient texts or practices can continue to be meaningful. There is no reason why the process should stop at any point. On the contrary, the freshness and relevance of the Gospel as Good News demands such a constant hermeneutic renewal.

Mystagogy is one of the elements that allows Rahner to make the fresh alliance between speculative and pastoral thinking which is one of his contributions to Catholic theological renewal. Mystagogy, as a pastoral/ spiritual factor, helped him bridge the centuries-wide gap between abstract theology and untheological spirituality.

Other theologians have followed the trail blazed by Rahner in attempting to find a spirituality adequate to the needs of Christians living in the world of today. Among these are Leonardo Boff and Edward Schillebeeckx.[18]

Although not using the language of mystagogy, another modern theologian sums up well the present situation of theological and pastoral need:

> The question of God for us today in the twentieth century, as distinct from any other century, is about the possibility of experiencing God in the world. Where do we experience God in this life? At what point(s) in human existence does the reality of God impinge on human experience? What are the basic ingredients of an experience of God? The mystery of God is not some kind of theorem to be proved; it is rather, an experience to be lived . . . God comes to man *in* experience. We receive God in experience. We do not project, create or posit God in experience. Rather we find God, already there ahead of us, in human experience.[19]

MYSTAGOGY IN SPIRITUAL THEOLOGY

The use of mystagogy, not to comment on the rites of initiation, but to draw out spiritual lessons for the Christian to experience the depths of the Mystery, dates back at least to Maximus the Confessor. Maximus himself had passed from an administrative career to the monastic life. He is seen as linking the two traditions, of liturgy and desert asceticism. The godparent or sponsor at baptism may be seen as a 'spiritual father'. The instruction Chrysostom gives to sponsors, in his second baptismal homily, speaks of them as spiritual guides to the neophytes.

The Desert Fathers insisted on what is now mostly called 'spiritual direction', and this has been recovered to be used in a revived 'mystagogy' in the area of spirituality. In addition to a spiritual father or guide, other elements of continuity between the spirituality of the Desert Fathers and of renewed mystagogy are noted: the contemplative or mystical strand, centred on the totality of the Mystery, and the primacy of experience.

The language of mystagogy, as taken up by theologians of mysticism, is not accessible to the sort of ordinary Christian of whom Rahner is thinking. The authors (mostly Italian) who currently use the language of mystagogy in their spiritual theology do not exclude those who are not members of 'Institutes of Perfection', but neither do they make much allowance for them in their language or in their descriptions of the path to be traversed in mystagogy. The caution given by Dermot Lane is in order here:

> Mystical experience should not be presented as the primary or principal experiential point of contact with God. Rather it is a possibility subsequent upon many and various other religious experiences.[20]

This is not to exclude the possibility of mysical experience in the strictest sense:

> It is at least possible that the individual, after undergoing many religious experiences, might momentarily disregard the medium disclosing the religious dimension of life and thus focus exclusively, *though darkly*, on the transcendent.[21]

Experience of God is fundamental to mystagogy and it is mystagogy which caters pastorally for the factor of experience in spirituality. Attempts to have people live an experience of God, as well as and in preference to gaining knowledge about God, have a tried and traditional pastoral instrument in mystagogy.

There remains the matter of the sound of the word. 'Mystagogy' is a word which easily evokes negative reactions from those who feel that anything which has to do with 'mystery', 'mysterious' or 'mystic' is necessarily out of touch with the real world in which normal people have to live their lives. The Enlightenment, whose gleams long thought themselves the only light in the universe and to whose star scientific people hitched their wagons, struggles against eclipse. Here it may only be possible to bring about a gradual change in mentality.

Vatican II, while not using the term 'mystagogy', does open the way for reintroduction of the practice through its pastoral orientation and through freeing theological thinking from slavery to categories of the past. Emphasis on the role of the Holy Spirit in the world and in the Church, insistence on the place of the Bible in theology and in the life of Christians, and renewal of liturgy, all served to inspire the search for an integrated spirituality. This spirituality would have a biblical base, be historical in outlook – as is the Bible – and have the forward-looking characteristic of the work of the Spirit. The pastoral emphasis of the Council, which found its clearest expression in *Gaudium et Spes* (the Pastoral Constitution on the Church in the Modern World), brought the everyday experience of contemporary men and women onto centre stage of the Church's spiritual concern. The joys, hopes, cares and sufferings of contemporary humanity must be the material for the Church's pastoral awareness. This document changed the way in which theology approaches its task, making pastoral service the noblest aim of theological speculation and constituting the experience of humanity as privileged starting-point for a theology and pastoral action which seek to overcome the threat of irrelevance.

In its treatment of the sanctity which is proper to all Christians, Vatican II stressed the role of the Holy Spirit and, without explicitly going into the question as to whether there is a universal call to mysticism, *Lumen Gentium* described Christian holiness in terms which recall the usual descriptions of the mystical. The Council leaves no doubt that all Christians are called to perfect holiness. Chapter five of *Lumen Gentium* is entitled 'De Universali Vocatione ad Sanctitatem in Ecclesia'. The text spells out what this means:

> The Lord Jesus, divine teacher and model of all perfection, preached holiness of life (of which he is the author and maker) to each and every one of his disciples without distinction: 'You, therefore, must be perfect, as your heavenly Father is perfect' (Mt. 5, 48). For he sent the Holy Spirit to all to move them interiorly to love God with their whole heart, with their whole soul, with their whole understanding, and with their whole strength, . . . and to love one another as Christ loved them . . . It is therefore quite clear that all Christians in any state or walk of life are called to the fullness of Christian life and to the perfection of love . . .[22]

The usual definitions of mystical life refer to the progressive taking over of control by the Holy Spirit through an ever greater motion of the gifts of the Spirit in the soul. This chapter five of *Lumen Gentium* does not say explicitly that this universal call to holiness means a call to the mystical life. Yet, each of the four paragraphs that make up the chapter speaks of holiness as the work of the Holy Spirit; in addition to the passage above it says:

> This holiness of the Church is constantly shown forth in the fruits of grace which the Spirit produces in the faithful . . . they are told by the apostle to live 'as is fitting among saints' (Eph. 5,3), and . . . to have the fruits of the Spirit for their sanctification . . . The forms and tasks of life are many but holiness is one – that sanctity which is cultivated by all who act under God's Spirit . . . God has poured out his love in our hearts through the Holy Spirit who has been given to us . . . therefore the first and most necessary gift is charity . . .[23]

Such frequent mention of the Holy Spirit as operating the work of holiness would seem to imply that the sort of control of the Christian's life by the

Spirit which is understood as 'mystical' can scarcely be a completely different path to holiness from that general one outlined by the Council. The mystical is not, therefore, outside of the concerns of the generality of Christians, and a pastoral practice which seeks to lead Christians to experience ever more deeply the Mystery to which they belong cannot prescind from mysticism.

I hesitate to suggest the use of the expression 'mystagogy' for individual spiritual direction. The writers who have worked in this direction – almost exclusively in Italy – have mostly retained a vocabulary which is not helpful today. The idea that to lead the individual into mystical experience through contemplative prayer is the perfection of mystagogy might pass, although it is not a patristic use of the expression. Today it would be more helpful to see mystical experience as attainable (not independently of prayer) in forms of spirituality integrated into life and activity for the salvation of aspects of our world. Animators and advisers to groups engaged in such pursuits could exercise a highly mystagogic function if they perceived the theologico-spiritual import of what they were about, appreciating the depths of the Mystery whose surface they were daily touching. This is spiritual direction too, but in a community setting and, as such, is better called mystagogy.

NOTES

1 Cf. D. Lane, *The Experience of God: An Invitation to do Theology* (Dublin: Veritas, 1981), p. 5.
2 Cf. *SC* 2.
3 *DV* 8.
4 *SC* 64.
5 *SC* 66.
6 *SC* 67.
7 When parish priest in Brazil in the 1960s, this author used the experimental rite with *Niseis* (young people born in Brazil to Japanese immigrant parents).
8 John A. Gurrieri, Executive Director of the Secretariat of the Bishops' Committee on the Liturgy, US National Conference of Catholic Bishops, in the Foreword to the Revised English text of *Christian Initiation of Adults* (Washington: USCC, 1988), p. 1.
9 RCIA 37–40.
10 RCIA 37; the English translation used throughout is that of the International Commission on English in the Liturgy (ICEL).
11 RCIA 38.
12 Pastoral periodicals keep in touch with developments in Christian initiation in the US and France: *Catechumenate*, a Chicago-based journal, having published more than a dozen volumes, tends to make mystagogy part of catechesis – cf. R. A. Oakham, 'Sowing for a good harvest: the underpinnings of mystagogy', vol. 12

(1990), pp. 22–7. In France, *Croissance de l'Eglise* is published by the Service Nationale du Catéchuménat.

13 RCIA 7d, 37–40. Faced with the Latin: *Ultimus tempus, quod per totum tempus paschale perdurat, attribuitur 'mystagogiae', id est* . . . ICEL translates thus: 'The final period extends through the whole Easter season and is devoted to the postbaptismal catechesis or mystagogy . . .'

14 Roman documents, compiled by committees of many members, occasionally show contrasting trends in their make-up. While one understanding of the matter formally prevails, traces of other ways of looking at it may survive the various editings.

15 K. Rahner, 'Christian living formerly and today' in *Theological Investigations* 7 (London: Darton, Longman & Todd, 1971), p. 15.

16 K. P. Fischer, *Gotteserfahrung: Mystagogie in der Theologie K. Rahners und in der Theologie der Befreiung* (Mainz: Mattias Grünewald, 1986), p. 29.

17 It does seem that Rahner lost heart in the future of his revival of the notion and language of mystagogy: his later works do not reveal any stress on the expression.

18 L. Boff, 'Experimentar a Deus Hoje' in various authors, *Experimentar Deus Hoje* (Petrópolis: Vozes, 1974), pp. 126–90; G. Siegwalt, 'Theologie systematique et mystagogique', *Revue d'Histoire et de Philosophie Religieuse* 62 (1982), pp. 251–9; E. Schillebeeckx, *Church: The Human Story of God* (London: SCM, 1990).

19 D. Lane, *The Experience of God*, pp. 2–3.

20 D. Lane, op. cit., p. 18.

21 Ibid.

22 *LG* 40.

23 *LG* 39–42.

3

MYSTAGOGY AND EXPERIENCE

Experience marks our Judeo-Christian tradition indelibly: from the Exodus to the Christ event, it is founded on religious experience. We ignore that experience at our peril. Each generation, collectively and individually, must recapture that foundational experience or face a crisis of identity. Pastoral structures must take account of that religious experience and cater for it. Such structures – notably mystagogy – existed in more holistic times; we could learn from them in our time of crisis.

Mystagogy always aimed at initiating men and women into an experience of the divine. Such initiation may have taken place in a House of the Mysteries of Greco-Roman mystery cults (under other names in the traditional religions of Africa and Asia), or in classical Christian times: the aim has always been to achieve a transforming experience for the candidate. Catholic theology in the West shied away from experience for a thousand years, so that to link experience and theology sounds strange. Yet, since it is in the context of experience that mystagogy operates, something must be said about it. This is made easier by the fact that experience is basic to contemporary Western culture.[1]

The Old Testament recounts the religious experience of Israel. That experience formed an ethnic mob into a people peculiarly God's own and led them forward on the course of that history which was to be vital for all humanity. Yahweh was known, not in philosophical argument, but in the experience of Israel's liberation from slavery in Egypt. Yahweh's covenant with Israel was celebrated in the dramatic Sinai experience, which marked the mediating, prophetic figure of Moses, and then the whole people.

Experience was responsible for the very name of God, since ancient Israelite belief in God was grounded in historical experience and developed in constant contact with history: so much is this true that the name Yahweh refers to a specific historical encounter.

Jesus had the most vivid experience of God, which he expressed – in his first and programmatic address – as an experience of the God who promised release for the captives, sight for the blind, liberation of the oppressed and a new year of jubilee (Luke 4:18–19). Jesus' perception was one of the imminence of the Kingdom of God (Mark 1:15) and of the experience of God present and active in his own prophetic person.[2] Jesus had also complete experience of the human condition:

> The mystery of the Incarnation and Redemption is . . . described as
> a total self-emptying which leads Christ to experience fully the
> human condition and to accept totally the Father's plan.[3]

Rigorous in application of the law of God, Jesus is, yet, sovereignly free in its interpretation. He has an experience of God that goes beyond the Law and, in consequence, he forbids anyone to make the Law an absolute. He experienced God as Father (*Abba*), full of faithfulness and love: a love that goes beyond all law and forbids any complacency about the fulfilment of precept. His own goodness and mercy is a translation of his experience of God as full of love and mercy and not a rigorous tyrant.

Jesus taught and acted with authority, due to the experience which he had of the Father and of the Spirit (John 15 – 17); this authority set him apart from other religious teachers and rulers (Matt 7:29). The Christian Church grew out of the religious experience that his disciples had of their master, Jesus freeing men and women and human society from shackles forged over the centuries. From the first day they heard the words 'Come and see; come with me' (cf. John 1:39; Mark 1:17), until they were filled with the Spirit at Pentecost, the Apostles had been bathed in the deep religious experience of accompanying Jesus while he was about his mission. What they had heard, seen, looked upon and touched with their hands, the disciples transmitted to their followers. This welded them into a fellowship, forged through sharing in Jesus' experience and his mission. Many years later, they recalled that experience with joy:

> That which was from the beginning, which we have heard, which we
> have seen with our eyes, which we have looked upon and touched
> with our hands, concerning the word of life . . . we proclaim also to
> you, so that you may have fellowship with us; and our fellowship is
> with the Father and with his Son Jesus Christ. And we are writing
> this that our joy may be complete. (1 John 1:1, 3–4)

Disciples remembered that experience of the word of life. The communities they founded (the Churches the Apostles left behind) eventually wrote down their reminiscences and reflections, giving us the New Testament. The founding experience was prior to all else. The moral imperative to live as Jesus did was a consequence of such experience and not a condition for having it. 'He who says he abides in him ought to walk in the same way in which he walked' (1 John 2:6); 'If then you have been raised with Christ, seek the things that are above . . .' (Col 3:1); 'We were buried therefore with him by baptism into death, so that as Christ was raised from the dead by the glory of the Father, we too might walk in newness of life' (Rom 6:4). The expressions used here by John: to 'abide in' Jesus Christ; or those used by Paul, in Romans 6, to be 'united with' Jesus in a death like his; to 'die with Christ' so as 'to live with him'; 'to be buried with him' by baptism, so as to be able to 'walk in newness of life', sound strange to ears accustomed only to 'objective', legalistic categories. These New Testament expressions have a mystical ring about them; they all presuppose some underlying religious experience. Paul had to invent terms to do justice to his own experience of being caught up into Christ to share in a common task and destiny with him. Paul's conversion experience on the road to Damascus shaped all his theology: the reality of the words, 'I am Jesus, whom you are persecuting' (Acts 9:5), left its mark on Paul's consciousness, revealing so close a unity between Christ and the Christian that it needed conversion to live it and new terms to express it.

The new terms in which Paul captured the original, holistic view of Christian faith were subsequently lost when an exclusively intellectual theology splintered the Christ event into a multitude of 'truths to be believed'. 'Mysteries of faith' were so multiplied that to speak of the 'Mystery of Christ' ceased to have meaning. Even today, three decades after Vatican II, talk of the Christian's baptismal 'insertion into the Mystery of Christ' is incomprehensible to many Catholics, even to those of more than average education – Paul's experience-based theology has scarcely been taught or preached for centuries, his mystical vision lost to arid intellectualism and peripheral devotion.[4]

Only now, helped by interest in renewal of the charismatic heritage of Christianity, is the element of experience being given its value in New Testament texts. In the letter to the Galatians, Paul is now seen as using the Christians' conversion experience of the Spirit as an argument for the superiority of their faith over the Law.[5] In recent translations of Galatians 3:1, the Greek word *paschō*, long rendered as 'suffer', is being given the less restricted meaning of 'experience': 'Did you receive the Spirit by works of the law, or by hearing with faith? Are you so foolish? Having begun with the Spirit, are you now ending with the flesh? Did you experience (*epathete*) so many things in vain? – if it really is in vain. Does he who supplies the Spirit to you and works miracles among you do so by works of the law, or by hearing with faith?' (Gal 3:2b–5). Contemporary Scripture studies see Paul using this passage to build an argument for the superiority of faith over the law. The meaning given to this one word seems crucial to the argument. In his commentary on Galatians, in *The New Jerome Biblical Commentary* (1990), Joseph Fitzmyer sees various instances of experience as so many proofs in Paul's argument, given in chapters 3 and 4, that 'In God's Plan Humanity is Saved by Faith, Not by the Law'. The first of these proofs is the 'Experience of the Galatians in First Receiving the Spirit (3:1–5); Proof 2: Experience of Abraham and God's Promises to Him (3:6–26); Proof 3: Experience of Christians in Baptism (3:27–29); Proof 4: Experience of Christians as Children of God (4:1–11); Proof 5: Experience of Galatians in Their Relation to Paul (4:12–20) . . .'[6]

A contemporary of Cyril of Jerusalem, Hilary, Bishop of Poitiers, in Gaul, poet and hymn-writer, had no doubt about the place of charisms in baptism. He took it for granted that something of what happened to Christ in the Jordan would happen to the neophyte in his or her baptism: 'We who have been reborn through the sacrament of baptism experience intense joy when we feel within us the first stirrings of the Holy Spirit.'[7]

Cyril of Jerusalem, in his first mystagogic homily, points out that what has been seen touches one more than what has only been heard about – what has been experienced rather than what has been taught abstractly. It is for this reason that he has waited until after the rites of initiation to explain their mystic signification.[8]

Cassian says that it is not reading which makes us penetrate the meaning of the words of the psalms we recite, but the spiritual experience that we have already gained and now bring to this exercise. Cassian frequented the solitaries in the desert who had learned about contemplation through experience rather than through abstract study.

Throughout the earlier patristic period, theology was still part of a whole which had not clearly distinguished the experiential from the intellectual, homiletics from theological speculation, praxis from theory. Each aspect of life was lived and seen as linked to and bound up with every other. This is characteristic of an oral culture, and Christians lived for centuries in an oral cultural milieu.

Church Councils were originally gatherings of representatives of all or part of the Christian people of God to discern the way forward in face of new religious experience. It was only later that such experiences were thought of in terms of doctrinal truth or falsehood.

When the doctrinal was emphasized to the detriment of the experience, damage was done to the tradition. Vatican II was convoked to consider the pastoral relevance of the Church's evangelizing operation in a changing world, and not to deal with some error of doctrine. It marked a return to concern with the way in which men and women experience religion. The cultural gap between contemporary religious experience and the language of preaching and teaching had grown so wide as to threaten the credibility of all the Church's pastoral action. To a great extent it still does.

Little valued in the ages when metaphysics was in honour, experience saw the importance given it parallel the rise of modern science, especially the sciences of the human; and the fortunes of experience fluctuated according to the emphases uppermost in each stage of the controversy between empirical and idealist trends in philosophy.

Early in the twentieth century, William James's Gifford Lectures[9] brought religious experience and psychology together in an empirical study that drew attention to the topic of *The Varieties of Religious Experience* in modern terms. James stressed the individual and subjective emotional aspect of experience, to the detriment of the social and community (ecclesial) dimension. Interest in psychology had led to exaggerations as to the role of the subjective in religious experience. A few years later, the Modernist movement produced ripples on the surface of Catholic life, and the reaction to it, disturbing waves. The matter of religious experience was central to the Modernist crisis. The reaction against 'Modernism' made the question of experience in religion taboo for decades and it was only gradually that Catholic theology could discuss it openly. For generations religious feeling was to remain suspect. The anti-modernist oath, imposing an exclusively 'objective' approach to faith, was long mandatory for office holders. In the 1940s, Ronald Knox wrote a history of *Enthusiasm* that was on the whole hostile to the concept. In the 1950s, the French theologian Jean Mouroux's positive and balanced book on *Christian Experience*[10] helped exorcize the demons.

Theology in the 1940s and 1950s began to treat of earthly realities, work and other themes which opened the way beyond a separation between grace and nature, theology and life. With the Second Vatican Council, experience, after an absence of centuries, was once more given its place in Catholic theology in the West. In the document on Revelation, *Dei Verbum*, Vatican II included 'the intimate sense of spiritual realities which (believers) experience', with the Magisterium and theological reflection, as one of the ways in which tradition progresses.[11] It also stressed the factor of spiritual experience in culture.[12] In this matter, as in so many others, the Council rolled back the mists of history.

Various factors contributed to influencing theology in the direction of greater openness to the element of experience:

- an impatience with words as attempts to express what is most important or decisive; 'the end of the ideologies' left words in poor repute;

- the loss of the 'old ways' of approaching God;

- impatience with a disincarnate spirituality;

- reaction against the position of those apologists who gave reason an excessive role in their theology;

- the weakening of polemical attitudes to the Reformers who based faith largely on religious experience;

- the search to understand all reality through faith, rather than simply to deepen the understanding of faith itself;

- a return to symbolism that allows the element of experience to be brought into a theological synthesis;

- the place of the electronic media, giving extension to the senses which were forgotten in the age of the book: this development brings experience to the fore again, in a role approaching that which it has in oral cultures;

- the breakdown of recognized systems of belief led to a 'profound convulsion of spiritual life', which, in turn, generated interest in the now ailing psyche and the subjective processes of modern man – a turning inward comparable only to the gnostic movement of the first centuries of the Christian era.

Carl Jung (to whom we owe the last point in the above list), analyses the crisis in spirituality of his time. He finds it to be due to the fact that religion no longer embraces life in its fullness: the hegemony over the psyche, formerly held by clergy, is passing. Jung thinks that this is an aspect of the normal cultural development of humanity and one towards which, in our case, natural science contributed. Man has also turned his attention to some extent from external things to examine his own psychic processes:

> modern man . . . turns his attention to the psyche with very great expectations . . . without reference to any traditional creed, but rather in the Gnostic sense of religious experience.[13]

Because the modern scientific mentality wishes to measure everything through controlled experience or experiment, it has become necessary to examine the hermeneutic of experience – how it helps us achieve real knowledge. We now know that our experience is not a passive mirroring which yields up purely objective knowing, but that any experience is conditioned by our existing heuristic models. We know with everything that we are and everything that we already know. The answers yielded by our experience depend on the questions we ask of it.

The prevailing culture is oriented towards experience, not towards principles and norms. Surveys on religion are beginning to research religious experience rather than beliefs or religious practice. To deal with religious experience, the post-Vatican II Church has not only adopted discernment in spiritual direction and pastoral planning, but has incorporated much of the wisdom of the psychological sciences into its spiritual theology.

Few Catholics today have patience with a highly intellectual theology, dogmatic about its conclusions. Security is sought, instead, in the more direct experience of the divine available in mysticism. An increasing number are reading the writings, not only of the classical mystical doctors of the Church, Teresa of Ávila and John of the Cross, but of other mystics, medieval and modern. Feeling that drugs ought not to be allowed a monopoly on ecstasy, others research and follow mystical currents in the great world religions.

Disillusion arising from the shortcomings of the modern culture of the Enlightenment is leading to a reaction against what is merely rational and to a rediscovery of the value of experience. Some prefer the name 'trans-modern' to 'post-modern' for this trend.[14] There are some signs that, even in big business corporations, older people, with a broad, humanistic training rather than narrow specialization, are being chosen for leadership positions in times of rapid change; the broad sweep of their experience fits them for adapting to change better than the specialist. We may recall that in pre-modern societies, especially ones of an oral culture, the elders were the depositaries of the memories of the group and their long experience of life gave them a spread of wisdom impossible to the young. They were societies in which specialization was minimal, but perhaps a trans-modern society must try to combine both the wisdom that comes from experience and the knowledge that comes from specialized study.

The *Ordo* for the Christian Initiation of Adults, of 1972, which formally restored mystagogy to the Church's official initiatory procedures, speaks of the neophytes undergoing the twofold experience of the sacraments and of the Church community.[15] The emphasis is distinctly on experience rather than on any intellectual content of the exposition. In the forty paragraphs of the main part of the RCIA, the expression 'experience' is employed on nine occasions, six of them in direct relation with the mystagogy, one in speaking of the precatechumenate, and two with reference to the catechumenate.

It was especially during the 1970s that theologians began to study the question of experience. The fruits of their studies have not yet been integrated into religious formation and in many places theology itself continues to be taught from an abstract and academic point of view, with little base in concrete experience. In a pluralist and multi-cultural world this leads to a form of clerical schizophrenia in the individual and to continued irrelevance at the pastoral level.

Theologians are, more and more, taking experience of concrete situations as starting-point for their reflection. For example, some feminist biblical scholars maintain that the divine intervention of the Exodus and later was experienced by the whole people, but consigned to writing only by males, so that it still remains to be discovered how a woman's experience of those events might have been articulated.

The knowledge which arises through experience is not mere sense perception of the object; nor is it a purely subjective impression. Experience is fruit of an encounter between a human subject and surrounding reality. It is not alien to thought; it involves thought as turned towards the presence of an object. It is the element of rational reflection that gives experience its human quality and makes it different from simple sense perception. Some emotion normally accompanies experience and a profound experience is usually accompanied by deep emotion, but emotion is not of itself the whole of experience. The interpretation of experience is always done from within the culture to which one belongs, even prior to any explicit appeal to the discernment of the community.

Human experience underlies religious experience, revelation and faith.[16] The Spirit of God is active in the whole universe and God is present to all. It is in common conviction as to fundamental values that the grace of God is discerned at work in the world. Such values include: life and the means to promote it; liberation from all that enslaves; respect for the integrity of creation. Reaction in faith to the special historical experience of the Exodus brought the people of Israel into being and gave rise to the covenant. The community's accounts of these events and of their significance for them brought the Old Testament Scriptures to birth. Jesus Christ in his person and witness to God as Father, and above all, in his death and resurrection, brought revelation to its peak and provided the historical experience that led his followers to a new strength of communion and witness to him.

It is in experience that the tension between theory and practice is resolved. It is easy to learn theories but difficult to put them into practice or to see their relevance and limitations for the sphere of practice. When our theological enterprise begins with an experience on which we want to build, it is possible to read the situation or event which has been experienced, and see in that concrete case the relevance and limitations of the theory. The Theology of Liberation starts from experience, especially the experience of the poor, and passes through a process of reflection producing a theory on which are based decisions directed to action. It is a theology closely related to pastoral or missionary action. Theory which is based on concepts abstracting from history and movement, and all experience of these, has great difficulty in coming to practical decisions for action in the concrete world. A theory easily arises which seems valid on its own terms but does not satisfy those who want motives for action.

In spite of the radical change towards experience in culture and the consequent adaptation in spirituality, the structures of religious formation have not changed. It is true that new dimensions have been explored in catechesis, attempting to provide a holistic approach to religion – including, at times, religious experience. But the old intellectual learning of truths has so marked the catechetical enterprise as a whole, that it rubs off on any mere change in perspective. Religious experience has not been explicitly recognized as a major value in Christian initiation and no new structure in religious formation has marked the change in cultural outlook. This is where mystagogy should come in: it is geared to experience, has links with initiation and is a practice which could easily mark a new pastoral structure.

Experience defines mystagogy, while all the rest – language, the guidance of a master, ascetical practices – are aimed at preparing, promoting or drawing fruit from the experience. Presence, wholeness and communion are aspects of spiritual experience . . . a communion of presence in which the subject as a whole takes to itself the object as a whole . . . In the case of transcendental realities this experience will normally be mediated through signs and symbols.[17] Of course, for many persons of modern mentality it is easy to discount religious experience as illusion and it was once fashionable to use psychoanalytic theories to justify this rejection.

Over the centuries, the Eastern tradition remained closer to the mystical and experiential in its theology than did the Christian West. Now, parallel to the rediscovery of the importance of experience, there is a return to Eastern sources on the part of theologians from the Western tradition.

It was a couple of years after the Council that Karl Rahner pointed out the need for some version of mystagogy – the pastoral practice of the patristic centuries for leading candidates for Christian faith to an experience of the Mystery of Christ. He addressed his updated version of mystagogy, not to new converts, but to men and women living in the world. The Rahner initiative did not catch on, perhaps because it lacked a structure for practical implementation.

The theology of Karl Rahner includes experience as an essential element. The content of the Christian message is tied to the elucidation of the mystery of the experience which the human person has of his or her own reality. The mystery of God, who gives himself in love, is the only key to the mystery of human experience. Without genuine inner experience, changing a man or woman, he or she falls into ideology. Rahner brings the experience element onto centre stage as necessary in today's pluralist world. There is need for a mysticism that leads to an experience of God in the darkness of modern living.

Rahner's project takes account of the needs of the modern lay person in the industrialized world. It is not a spirituality for professional contemplatives, nor a way of pure interiority, like customary types of mysticism lived far from the paths of history. It passes through the individual and collective history of humankind's transcendental nature and therefore caters for the 'worldliness' of the life which these Christians have, by vocation, to live.

Our times are bounded by a technico-scientific horizon. Science and technology, not mysticism or metaphysics, have until recently marked the dominant culture and mentality. But God is not an object to be experienced directly like other objects; he emerges from the radical nature of our experience of the world. More recent theologians would add that only where we allow such experience to be open, and not imprisoned in *a priori* rationalist categories, can it become radical and include the more than rational roots of the universe, and the Mystery.

Edward Schillebeeckx, too, finds a new approach to theology through starting from experience. Not theory, but experience, is the starting-point for approaching the religious question today. The 'interpretative *a priori*' is not the search for ultimate meaning, but is to be found in the experience of saying 'no' to evil, suffering, oppression, injustice. Many intuitions of the Liberation theologians are accepted here. Evil is to be found, not just in individual lives, but in the structures of society. Jesus' practice in favour of the coming of the Kingdom, and not his theory, becomes the yardstick for fidelity.[18]

Leonardo Boff maintains that an over-exclusive affirmation of divine transcendence led to a denial of the world; exclusive emphasis on immanence led to a denial of God, while the world was affirmed. God is not just transcendent and he is not just immanent, he is transparent, as Paul says in Ephesians 4:6: 'One God and Father of us all, who is above all (transcendent), and through all (transparent) and in all (immanent)'.

This divine transparency is there for the seeking, in 'ordinary' situations of human life:

> God is not 'visible' and 'audible' and 'accessible', in mystical experience alone. If this were the case, God would be the privileged luxury of some few initiates and not the Meaning which pervades all existence, even the most ordinary . . . How can this experience of God be realized in one's personal journey? Is there some sort of mystagogy? . . . Each one, on life's journey, has to discover by experience the roots which nourish his life.[19]

God can be known through every experience of another human being. Each human person is a mystery and each one sounds different depths of that mystery as going through life we ask ourselves what it means to be human. The answers we get to that question are lost in the great Mystery which is God. In the mystery of man is situated the ontological ground for the identification made by Christ between love of neighbour and love of God. Loving another profoundly, we achieve love of God. Boff continues:

> We could go on indefinitely analysing the existential situations of man in which the totally other may be seen, Mystery, Meaning, complete openness to the future, gratuitousness in life, the demand for an absolute Thou. All these experiences, which occur in daily living, are really expressions of the one unifying human experience which we call God.[20]

In a recent article, Boff develops the theology of ecology and speaks of the transparency of the world to the Mystery:

> That the world regain its enchantment, it is not enough to wish it to be so; we have to broaden our horizons beyond those of modern rationalism and become aware, symbolically and mystically, that the world carries a message and a mystery. This mystery is glimpsed both by scientists who push their knowledge of matter, energy and life to the limit and by mystics, of East and West, who see the world as a system of acting and reacting energies, in movement and integration and involving the supreme Spirit who penetrates the whole, conferring life and transparency.[21]

Experience, being subjective and personal, is liable to be misinterpreted: there is need for some method of judging the validity of what claims to be Christian experience. It is not coincidence that the return of 'experience' as a factor in theology has been accompanied by a growth in 'discernment'.

New situations in the past gave rise to structures of discernment. Aids to discernment were developed over the Christian centuries: for the individual monk, the safeguard of a spiritual father was deemed advisable; for the cenobitic institution, a rule helped avoid imprudences and error. The reading of experience at ecclesial level requires communion, dialogue and the loyal co-operation of many. Pelagius and Luther are cited as examples of people who had genuine spiritual experiences, but who failed to situate these experiences in the context of a total theological and ecclesial view.[22] The constant need for discernment is evident, especially when dealing with new spirituality, new theology or new ecclesial structures.

If doctrine is not the whole of Catholicism, but experience is part of it too, how are we to avoid a free-for-all, do-it-yourself, ready-mix religion? Once anything other than the utterly objective is admitted, the 'modern' mind calls for some mechanism for evaluating such experience. To be authentic, the religious experience of the individual Christian must, in some measure, resemble that of Christ. Church authorities can control doctrine, but how is experience to be authenticated? At the same time that religious experience came in again to the theological orbit, ways were found for evaluating it. To have social value, subjective experience must pass some test.

From his perspective, William James, while regaling his audience with what he considered extreme examples of religious experience, was careful to promise, from the outset, that he would later submit these experiences to what was for him the ultimate test, that of common sense:

> Such convulsions of piety, they will say, are not sane. If, however, they will have the patience to read to the end, I believe that this unfavorable impression will disappear; for I there combine the religious impulses with other principles of common sense which serve as correctives of exaggeration, and allow the individual reader to draw as moderate conclusions as he will.[23]

Techniques for Christian discernment of spirits are gradually being developed or rediscovered, more usually for individual use, but also, if more slowly, for community use; because religious experience is a phenomenon not only of individuals but of groups and peoples, too. In spirituality – which for so long was exiled from a theology which had no place for experience of God and the things of God – discernment of spirits was never quite forgotten, masters of the art, such as Ignatius of Loyola and Francis Libermann, providing guidance.

Theology now recognizes that the community itself is subject of religious experiences, especially in real liturgy (as distinct from merely repetitive ritual), and the community plays an inescapable role in the interpreting of the experiences of individuals. This happens, not just explicitly, when the experiences are brought to the community for formal evaluation, but also at a deeper level. All experience, the religious included, is interpreted with the help of the community or prevailing culture. The individual cannot escape the influence of family and community background in the interpretation he or she gives to what is experienced. The community is there as third party in the process of experiencing. With the insight gained from later studies we can see that James's 'scientific' stance of treating religious experience from the viewpoint of the individual alone (and leaving it only to individuals to evaluate accounts of such experiences), effectively mutilated the experiences through ignoring the prime hermeneutic factors of the prevailing culture and the concrete community to which the individual belongs.

Israel had its prophets. Filled with the Spirit, when necessary they 'blew the whistle' on exaggerations or deviations in the practical interpretation of the Exodus and other experiences. Prophetic intervention was the usual regulatory mechanism. Any institutional structure, other than the Torah (Books of the Law) itself, for the authoritative interpretation of new religious experiences was of very late introduction in Judaism.[24] Such interpreting, when it occurred, was just that, the best hermeneutic available for understanding the relevance of the foundation-experience to new situations. Interpreting of experience is still largely the function of theological reflection and authority in the Judeo-Christian tradition. Prophetic intervention questions the monopoly which the religious authorities tend to exercise in the matter. Excoriated by contemporary religious authorities, to be venerated by later generations (Matt 23:29f.; Luke 11:47), is the prophetic lot; Jesus himself was no exception.

The Irish theologian Dermot Lane[25] provides a series of criteria for evaluating religious experience. Derived from Schillebeeckx, Tracy, Ogden and Gilkey, these criteria may be summed up in the key words underlined by Lane: *commitment, decision, conversion, continuity* and *compatibility*. The proposed criteria must answer the requirement that the religious dimension of experience meet the demands of modern secular life. On the other hand the religious interpretation of experience must be faithful to the demands of a specifically Christian understanding of existence:

1 The transcendent reality disclosed (in the experience) must be consonant with the incarnational revelation of God as Father in the person of his Son Jesus Christ through the power of the Holy Spirit. The experience must bring about a real *commitment* to the person of Jesus as the Christ who is the Word of God made flesh.

2 The religious experience would have to result in *decision* inspired and informed by the vision of Christ. Such decision would be influenced by the teaching of Jesus about realities like the kingdom of God, the Beatitudes and the new commandment of love.

3 The nature of the *conversion* would have to be both paschal and practical. It would have to be paschal by being patterned on the saving death and resurrection of Jesus which brought newness of life through death. It would have to be practical in terms of bringing about a transformation of the individual and society in the service of the kingdom of God: 'You will know them by their fruits' (Mt 7:20).

4 The religious experience would need to exist in some form of *continuity* with the experience of the Christian community as expressed in Sacred Scripture and transmitted in the living tradition of that community. The task of determining this would rest with the recognized authority that resides within the Christian community.

5 The meaning of the religious experience would have to be *compatible* with the established Christian *regula fidei*. It would have to fit in, at least with the hierarchy of truths and values that exists within Christianity.

6   The truth implicit in the religious experience would have to harmonize
    with the eschatological understanding of reality that is specific to
    Christianity. This would embrace the promise of a new heaven and a new
    earth centred in the kingdom of God to come. (pp. 26–7)

Symbols, so widely used in liturgy, do justice to experience in a way that
doctrinal concepts cannot. The sacramental order of the Church is based on
symbolism and this is why it is capable of leading to the divine without
falsifying what it symbolizes. The abandoning of symbolism in favour of a
more dialectic – philosophy-based – theology accompanied the medieval loss
of mystagogy and favoured stress on the distinction between the natural and
supernatural orders.[26]

   Use of symbolism accounts for the poetry of biblical texts, and early
theology largely consisted in an investigation of the symbolic language used in
Scripture. The philosophical limitations of this (typological) method, led to
adopting more intellectually exact procedures. Definition of terms and the
application of logic soon left no room for the poetic, the mythical or the
mystic. Together with the rediscovery of the importance of what is seen,
heard, felt and imagined, there comes today a return of interest in myth, in
religious poetry and in Eastern and Western mysticism. Père Gy, the
liturgist, quotes P. Duployé's explanation of the poetic language of
Ambrose's *De mysteriis*:

> In these texts, there is more than the joy of the truth, there is delight
> in the truth . . . Love sings . . . In Ambrose's text there is no explicit
> reflection on the mystery, only the starkest presentation possible, but
> there is an intense fervour and mystery. It is a purely poetical text
> . . . Mystagogical texts speak prophetically about things prophetic;
> imaginatively about things of the imagination; . . . poetically about
> things poetic and mysteriously about mysteries.[27]

Gy asks whether mystagogic texts are necessarily poetic. He does not answer.
   Treating of symbolism, a modern theologian has written:

> Symbol has the power to evoke mystery. Mystery ultimately lies in
> God's intention and power, but mediately in human history and
> experience.
> Symbol has power to evoke mystery because it addresses itself to the
> whole person – to the imagination, the will, and the emotions, as well
> as to the intellect – and because it is deeply rooted in human
> experience and human history. One cannot simply invent true
> symbols. They emerge from the depths of human consciousness,
> both individual and collective, and they last as living symbols only as
> long as they continue to evoke those depths.[28]

Liturgy is woven from symbols. An understanding of how symbols work in structuring liturgy is needed to lead others into a fruitful participation in liturgical experience. To do justice to religious experience and the symbols which capture this, the liturgical mystagogue must attend to three things:
(a) the liturgical rite itself;
(b) the actual situation of those being initiated, their relation to the world in which they live;
(c) the material which can best give their deepest meaning to the symbolic words and gestures of the liturgy for these specific neophytes.[29]

New experiences, accompanying new situations of challenge to Christian faith, require new symbols, or new meanings to be attached to old symbols and images. This 'reading' of new experiences in the light of tradition is a hermeneutic process calling for creativity and prophetic charism. Reading symbols and the experience behind them calls for discernment, to do justice to the new reality and to Christian tradition.[30] In this way, the age of experience must also be the age of the Spirit. For experience to be positive, the role of the Spirit must be appreciated and the action of the Spirit discerned. This discernment is done by the individual and also by the community, local and wider. The freedom allowed the Spirit in the individual and in the local community poses a threat to leaders in the authoritarian mode. A conversion is called for so that decentralization may allow discernment of experience at local level to take over from centralized juridical control of everything. This is possible only where there is, on the part of all concerned, real faith in the action of the Holy Spirit in every Christian community.

The pastoral age is learning to handle experience theologically. The mystical meets the theoretical in a theology starting from experience. Action based on the evaluation of experience in the light of the word of God respects the initiative of the Spirit in the world, in individual hearts and in the local community. Discernment of the action of the Spirit becomes central to pastoral and missiological planning.

Basic ecclesial communities experience the mystery of God operative in their lives when they follow their own 'see, judge, act' pedagogy. Experience of their lives is the starting-point; reflection in faith – which becomes prayer – is the catalyst; and action to have their lives change so as to do justice to the image of God in which they were created is the goal. Systematically trampled on by all the agents of a particularly savage brand of capitalism, these people have little self-respect left them; they have long interiorized the contempt with which the privileged regard them. They have come to believe the myths woven by their oppressors to justify the structures of exploitation which lie upon them with the weight of centuries of slavery, low wages, substandard housing and lack of access to the ladder of social ascent: lazy, incapable of abstract thought, sexually irresponsible, less sensitive to heat and cold, hunger and thirst, than the master race, unsuited to higher education for clerical or professional avocations, and so on.

In biblical reflection, they discover that, throughout history, God has constantly shown himself on the side of the oppressed – that the very name of God is that of the One who liberated his people from slavery. The example of Jesus Christ allows them to feel God's closeness to them in their troubles. Jesus was born among the poor, although of royal lineage, and experienced, from the outset, hatred and jealousy, forced migration and exile, the opposition of the powerful in 'Church, State and the academic community', ostracism, false accusations, venal tribunal, torture and unjust death. For people of a fundamentally oral culture, little given to dividing life into religious and secular, this Gospel parallel to their own lives produces a powerful experience of closeness to the central Mystery of their Christian faith.

The example of a people in the Old Testament brings the courage and religious support needed to organize as a community, and network of communities, to work politically to bring about change in the oppression which they now see to be sinful and which they feel a God-given call to change. They perceive that the image of God in which they were created has been stamped out, and with mixed delight and terror they discover that they have an obligation to rise up against this state of affairs. God's holiness, if not their own interest, obliges them to go out from the relative security and known misery of their enslavement and set out on the arduous way through unknown deserts in search of a better land. They have discovered that, while their trust must be in God alone, they also have responsibility for writing the page of their own history – a history which is to be salvific, not only for themselves, but for their oppressors too.

The mystery of God's action in favour of his people, revealed in Old and New Testaments, casts a new light on the daily experience of illness, misery and struggle to survive. As communities grow into a new people, through organizing for their own liberation, they experience the Mystery of Christ's presence and the strength of his Spirit guiding their novice steps. Action and experience of God grow side by side: it is only experience of the mystery of God's liberating light and power that gives them the courage to struggle on and face the indifference of politicians and the fierce opposition of those who have a vested interest in maintaining an abundant source of cheap labour. Experience of the cross of Christ is near, in the violence of paid hirelings (official and other), paid to defend the interests of the rich minority, alive to any threat to the political, economic and cultural structures which guarantee their privileges.

An understanding of the extent to which the Mystery of Christ penetrates the history of this world – into which he entered once for all – gives a new possibility of a mystagogy embracing social, political and historical aspects of life, and finds in these material for an experience which is also integrally religious. This 'reading' of the experience of the poor is itself mystagogic. It is fruit of a theology which takes account of daily experience and shows how it is material for spirituality and transparent to the Mystery.

In patristic mystagogy, events of the Old Testament were employed as typological 'figures' of the New; but here – in the Theology of Liberation – the New Testament is presented in full historical continuity with the Old and in theological consistency with the present stage of salvation history, in continuity with both Testaments. At a national-level meeting of basic communities, in Vitoria, in the State of Espirito Santo, Brazil, in 1975, in simple words and images, a community member voiced this theological intuition:

> The Old Testament was written by an oppressed people. The New Testament, by the life of Jesus, a poor man from Nazareth, and by the lives of the apostles, all of them poor. We, the poor people of today, with our lives, are writing the Newest Testament.[31]

Basic communities provide, naturally and not by any artifice beyond the method which they use, a life-changing experience which is psychological – to the point of transforming personalities – powerfully political and integrally religious. The religious knowledge gained through the experience is rarely in terms which can be articulated – though, as in the above quotation, it can sometimes be articulated with simple brilliance – but is part and parcel of a profound conversion experience at the level of the individual and of the group. If and when the experience is articulated, this may be done – as in the above case – by a piece of original theological thinking, rather than through the reciting of texts memorized from someone else's theology. This is mystagogy rather than catechetics – a living approach to the Mystery, assimilated on one's own terms – rather than an intellectual learning of 'truths', in someone else's thought or language. This freedom granted the Spirit frightens those who want to control, if not all religious experience, at least its expression and interpretation.

NOTES

1 An example of how far experience has taken over from more metaphysical considerations in the practical affairs of people today is seen in the understanding of what constitutes a human person, as illustrated in the popular approach to the issue of abortion. Abstract definitions of what constitutes the human seem to have little weight as against the concrete experience of knowing some being as a

relating, responding individual. Unless this concrete experiential knowing has taken place, men and women of today do not easily accept that they are dealing with a person: the facility with which horrible deaths are inflicted on the unborn in the womb contrasts with the indignation at any degree of suffering inflicted on an animal which is known and loved as an individual. On the other hand, metaphysical considerations as to the dignity of the human person and the equality of all humans before God did not, for centuries, prevent the practice of discrimination against women.

2   L. Boff, 'Experimentar a Deus Hoje' in various authors, *Experimentar Deus Hoje* (Petrópolis: Vozes, 1974), pp. 162f.

3   John Paul II, *Redemptoris Missio* (1990), 88.

4   Unlike Catholic theology, Protestant theology continued to give experience a central place.

5   K. McDonnell and G. T. Montague, *Christian Initiation and Baptism in the Holy Spirit* (Collegeville, MN: Liturgical Press, 1991), p. 47. These authors repeatedly (pp. 77, 324) quote E. Schweizer's opinion, given in his Kittel article on the Spirit (*pneuma*), that: 'Long before the Spirit was a theme of doctrine, He was a fact in the experience of the community'. Surprisingly, for a rich study of 'Evidence from the first eight centuries', the authors do not include any reference to mystagogy in their final, pastoral recommendations.

6   *The New Jerome Biblical Commentary* (Englewood Cliffs, NJ: Prentice Hall/London: Geoffrey Chapman, 1990), p. 782.

7   Hilary of Poitiers, *Treatise on the Psalms*, quoted in K. McDonnell and G. T. Montague, *Christian Initiation*, p. 151.

8   Cyril of Jerusalem, *Catechism* XIX, 1.

9   W. James, *The Varieties of Religious Experience* (original edition, 1902; repr. Harmondsworth: Penguin, 1982).

10 J. Mouroux, *L'Expérience Chrétienne* (Paris: Aubier, 1954).

11 *DV* 8:

> Haec quae est ab Apostolis Traditio sub assistentia Spiritus Sancti in Ecclesia proficit: crescit enim tam rerum quam verborum traditorum perceptio, tum ex contemplatione et studio credentium, qui ea conferunt in corde suo . . . tum ex intima spiritualium rerum quam experiuntur intelligentia, tum ex praeconio eorum qui cum episcopatus successione charisma veritatis certum acceperunt.

12 *LG* 53.

13 C. G. Jung, 'The spiritual problem of modern man' in *Modern Man in Search of a Soul*, trans. from German (New York: Harcourt Brace, 1933), p. 207. William James would, doubtless, be one of these modern men.

14 Cf. the recent writings of Enrique Dussel, for an explanation of the term 'transmodern'.

15 Sacred Congregation for Divine Worship, *Ordo initiationis christianae adultorum*, *Notitiae* 8 (1972), 37–40.

16 Cf. W. James, *The Varieties of Religious Experience*; D. Lane, *The Experience of God: An Invitation to do Theology* (Dublin: Veritas, 1981); D. Tracy, *The Analogical Imagination* (London: SCM, 1981); E. Schillebeeckx, *Church: The Human Story of God* (London: SCM, 1990).

17 H. C. de Lima Vaz, 'A experiéncia de Deus' in *Experimentar Deus Hoje*, pp. 74–89, holds a definition of experience of God that places it outside the field of 'religious experience', which, in his view, belongs to the mythical and ahistorical.

God is experienced as the radical Meaning of everything and is thus, for someone who has faith, so experienced along with each experience of everything else.

18 E. Schillebeeckx, *Church*, pp. 15–45.

19 L. Boff, 'Experimentar a Deus Hoje', pp. 153–4 (translation mine): '. . . Como se faz esta experiência de Deus na caminhada pessoal? Pode existir uma espécie de mistagogia?'

20 Ibid., p. 160.

21 L. Boff, 'Religión, justicia societaria y reencantamiento de la creación', *Pasos* (Costa Rica), no. 45 (January/February 1993), p. 9.

22 M. Dupuy, 'Expérience et théologie', *NRT* 86 (1964), pp. 1154–5.

23 W. James, *The Varieties of Religious Experience*, Preface, p. xxxvi.

24 Cf. P. D. Hanson, *The People Called* (San Francisco: Harper and Row, 1987), pp. 167; 372f.

25 D. A. Lane, *The Experience of God*, pp. 22f.

26 Cf. J. A. Komonchak, 'Theology and culture at mid-century: the example of Henri de Lubac', *TS* 51 (1990), p. 584.

27 P.-M. Gy, 'La mystagogie dans la liturgie ancienne et dans la pensée liturgique d'aujourd'hui' in A. M. Triacca and A. Pistoia (eds), *Mystagogie: Pensée liturgique d'aujourd'hui et liturgie ancienne* (Rome: Edizioni Liturgiche, 1993), p. 139, quoting P. Duployé, *Les Origines du Centre de Pastorale Liturgique* (Mulhouse, 1968).

28 M. L. Cook, 'Revelation as metaphoric process', *TS* 47 (1986), pp. 391–2.

29 Cf. H. M. Riley, *Christian Initiation: A Comparative Study of the Interpretations of the Baptismal Liturgy in the Mystagogical Writings of Cyril of Jerusalem, John Chrysostom, Theodore of Mopsuestia and Ambrose of Milan* (Washington: Catholic University of America Press, 1974), p. 19.

30 E. Schillebeeckx, *Church*, p. 21.

31 Original in *SEDOC* (Petrópolis), vol. 7, cols 1066–8; translation mine.

4

MYSTAGOGY AND THE WORD OF GOD

Bible and liturgy are the two great starting-points for classic Christian mystagogy. The relationship between Old and New Testaments which the Fathers had in the fourth century is one key to the reading of their mystagogic homilies; the pastoral art, just then emerging, of interpreting the symbolism of the liturgy is the other. A brief look at each of these may help understand the patristic mystagogues. Chapter 4 will look at the biblical question of the use of the Word of God; Chapter 5 will consider liturgy in mystagogy.

Now that we are getting beyond scholastic theology it is possible to appreciate poetic aspects of the Bible. If life is larger than logic, it is also larger than all scientific approaches. The Mystery which underlies life and the whole universe is not accessible to merely philosophical analysis any more than it was to physics and chemistry. New-found respect for mythological ways of thinking and for forms typical of oral communication makes it easier to appreciate the transparency of the world to the divine. Our Christian and Catholic tradition has still more than enough of the doctrinal in it to safeguard against excess in the recovery of the poetic in religion.

In order to talk about invisible realities in a meaningful way we have to use symbols. All our language has symbols behind it:

> Language on the level of symbol–metaphor–story is primary, and language on the level of description and/or definition is secondary, subordinate but indispensable to the primacy of symbol. Symbolic experience that comes to metaphorical expression is the primordial

way of being human, because it touches upon and seeks to give expression to that which is rooted in the deepest mysteries of life, including our relationship to God, to self, to others in society, to our bodies, and to the whole of nature. We live within symbol as the prelinguistic bonding of ourselves to the cosmos.[1]

When the Church Fathers explained to the neophytes the Mystery into which they were being initiated, they used the relationship between the Old and New Testaments in a symbolic manner, giving especial attention to the texts used in the liturgy of the sacramental celebration of initiation. Liturgy, being made up of sacred objects, actions and gestures, as well as words, lends itself to wide interpretation of these symbols it uses. When the origins of rites or objects have been forgotten, the interpretation can become far-fetched and even fantastic. 'Spiritual' interpretations are then drawn out of happenings of the Old or New Testaments which had no remote historical connection with the new 'meaning'. This happens most easily with allegory. Allegory involves the rereading of an (Old Testament) event so as to have it illustrate some Christian principle. Paul uses it on occasion, even saying that he is doing so. Thus, in Galatians 4:21–31, Paul uses the story of Abraham's two sons – one born of his wife and the other of a slave girl – to compare the situation of Christians, who live in the new freedom gained by Jesus Christ, with that of the Old Testament Jews, whom he saw as slaves to the Law.

Some of the patristic mystagogues used this allegorical method to weave spiritual interpretations around the way the deacon wore his stole or the splendour of the bishop's garment (which was seen as symbolizing the next life). Most of these interpretations had some basis in the culture of the time. Others involved the application of the meaning of an historical event to another event with significance only to the eyes of faith. As Hugh Riley says, summing up his study of the patristic, liturgical mystagogy of the rites of initiation:

> Our study of the mystagogical interpretation of this rite has shown that natural symbol and contemporary cultural symbol have been related in an unforced way to the liturgical drama itself to reveal its meaning and that the use of the biblical framework of salvation history has been the guiding principle used to illumine the drama in its ultimate religious meaning, the presence in the liturgy of God's own activity.[2]

Allegory is so flexible a method that it allows all sorts of pious meaning to be applied to virtually any Old or New Testament event.

A simple conviction of faith underlies even the most apparently arbitrary medieval examples of liturgical allegorizing. The conviction, for example, that the Eucharist was the celebration of Christ's passion and death. The apparently arbitrary relating of liturgical facts to the passion was based on this underlying conviction which saw each gesture of the eucharistic prayer of the Roman Rite as allegorically related to some event of Christ's passion. When, for instance, the celebrant raised his voice during the latter part of the Canon of the Mass – apparently with the functional purpose of alerting the other ministers that it was time to begin dividing the consecrated bread – the allegorists saw this as the cry of the centurion standing at the foot of the cross, 'Truly this was the Son of God'. This 'meaning', given to the only liturgical element impinging on the consciousness of the participating laity for quite some minutes, had its devotional explanation in the underlying liturgical conviction that the Mass was all about Christ's passion – a conviction which was theologically accurate, if incomplete. It was a weak mystagogical expedient at a time when historical knowledge of the origin of the rites was at a low ebb.[3] It was abuse of this sort of allegorizing which led all figurative interpretation into disrepute, helped the demise of mystagogy and encouraged the early Reformers to ban all more-than-literal interpretation of the Bible.

In some cases, the Old Testament symbols: personages, actions and objects, are, later in the Bible, replaced by other realities. The symbols are then called 'types', the reality being called 'antitype' of the symbol it has replaced. In this way, Moses and David are seen as 'types' of Christ and the crossing of the Red Sea a type of baptism. The most authentic examples of this use of typology are found in the New Testament. 'Type' and 'allegory' are two quite different things.

The Antioch school of exegesis, reacting against exaggerations in the use of allegory, developed typology, not only in relation to the Old Testament, but also in explanation of the symbolism of the liturgy. The problem with typology is to know what Old Testament events or figures were 'types' of New Testament characters or events and to know what objects or actions were types of Christian liturgical ones. Old Testament events and personages which the New Testament relates typologically to Christ or Christian realities are privileged.

Although the Fathers used the Old Testament to help understand Jesus and his work, they did not start from the Old Testament, but from Christ. The conviction in faith from which they started was that the Old Testament could only be speaking about Christ. Their relating of the two Testaments was based on this simple conviction of Christian faith. The rest was a consequence of this.

Several biblical themes are popular with the patristic mystagogues: the Pauline theme of Christ the New Adam, in whose image man is (re-)created; the theme of a new baptismal Exodus in which freedom from slavery to sin and Satan is achieved in Christ; the theme, dating back to the Old Testament, of Israel the Spouse of Yahweh, now become the Church, Bride of Christ. A look at these themes and a sample of the patristic homilies which used them may give the flavour of mystagogic preaching.

One of the main biblical themes, fundamental to mystagogy, is that of man and woman created in the 'image of God'.[4] For Paul, Christ is the Second Adam, or rather, the Last Adam, the heavenly human whose radiant image we are all called to put on as we have all too long borne the image of Adam, our first father. The theme has, already in Paul, a baptismal application: in Romans 6:6, Paul tells the Christians that through baptism they share in Christ's death and resurrection: 'We know that our old self was crucified with him so that the sinful body might be destroyed, and we might no longer be enslaved to sin.' The 'old self' is the remains in us of the first Adam.

In the Fathers, this theme of man as image of God is exploited with the help of Greek philosophy. Plato had given weight to the notion of the 'divine in us' – the connaturality of the human soul with the divine – and his influence with the Greek Fathers was great. For Oriental Christians, the human is created in the 'image of God', that is, with the grace of God; so that charity, faith, virtue and *gnōsis* (knowledge) properly belong to him – sin is always contrary to his nature. There was not agreement as to whether humans were in the image of God through their spirit alone or as a composite whole, Origen maintaining the former and Maximus the Confessor, among others, the latter position.

The theme of the image of God is used by Cyril of Jerusalem in his third mystagogic sermon; the theme becomes mystagogic when it is used of the white robe of the newly baptized to express their resemblance to the glorified Christ. Indeed, the white robe is sometimes used also (notably in Ambrose and Chrysostom) as a bridal symbol of the new members of the Church, Bride of Christ.

The theology of the Eastern Churches today still holds the image or *icon* in great honour. It is the Holy Spirit who rescues the sullied image of Christ from our murky depths and works to have Christ born in our hearts through conversion and baptism, in a process which continues throughout life, until we become grown up in Christ.[5]

If the theme of man or woman in God's image belongs more obviously with the mystagogy of the post-baptismal rites, that of the newly won freedom from slavery belongs with the earlier Rite of Renunciation and Profession of Faith. Of this aspect of the rite, Riley says:

> The very choice of such a culturally meaningful symbol as slavery and freedom, which runs through so much of the mystagogy . . . shows how strongly the fathers saw the inextricable intertwinement between commitment to Christ and its social repercussions in one's context of life . . . The dimensions of these human problems are

made more acute precisely by revealing the deeper religious dimensions inherent in them. This the mystagogy does by combining cultural symbol with biblical material. Underlying this mystagogy are demands which would startle (and please) even the most enthusiastic and 'radical' of the modern social apostles. As a matter of fact, the radical demands which such apostles today make on the church are, in the light of this patristic mystagogy of the rejection of Satan and the commitment to Christ anything but far-fetched.[6]

The Paschal event, in whose celebration the catechumens are initiated into the Mystery of Christ, takes place on the anniversary of the Exodus. It was no coincidence that the annual celebration of the liberation of the Israelites, under Moses, from slavery to Pharaoh in Egypt should have become the Christian Easter. Christ's victory over Satan and death – his passover from death to life – took place during the Paschal feast in Jerusalem. The Exodus, in which the Israelites became a people (and at Sinai became the People of God), is foundation feast of Israel – national and religious festival together. The Exodus is the centre and focal point of the Old Testament, as the Kingdom won by Christ's Paschal Mystery is centre of the New; the former is type and promise of the latter and has its baptismal application to Christians and its place in their eucharistic celebration.

In our own times, whenever a people of the Judeo-Christian tradition is suffering oppression and seeks freedom, the language of Exodus gives them courage: 'Let My People Go', 'The Cry of the Poor', 'Easter Week' are rallying cries which echo this theme.

Christians are God's children, as were the Israelites before them, because of the nuptials of Yahweh with his Bride Israel and of Christ with his Bride the Church. Amos, Jeremiah and Ezekiel spoke of this theme, which was also seen to be celebrated by the Song of Songs. As well as having baptismal links, the theme belongs directly to the mystagogy of marriage.

Another pastoral application of the Word of God which has mystagogic potential is an old and traditional way of reading Scripture as spiritual nourishment. Beginning in patristic times, and with roots in Israelitic piety, the practice of *lectio divina* has, in one form or another, been a constant in Christian spirituality over the ages. Although often presented as an ascetical practice it can also, and more rightly perhaps, be considered mystagogical: the gratuitous, peaceful reading, at set times, preferably during the morning hours, and with attention to savouring the sweetness of the Spirit, bears mystagogic characteristics of leading the Christian into the depths of an experience of the Mystery.

Biblical theology today, insisting on the central place of the Exodus in the Old Testament and of Christ's Paschal Mystery in the New, makes it possible to give, once more, a mystagogic reading of Scripture. For many years, a verbal exegesis did not easily allow of reading biblical texts so as to see in them the relevance of the Mystery of Christ for our times. Theological insistence on the centrality of the Trinity made little sense of the liturgical position given to the Mystery of Christ. Division of Christian truth into a multitude of 'mysteries of faith', to each of which equal assent of faith was due, robbed mystagogy of any powerful centre into which to introduce newcomers to the faith. The elimination of the element of experience from theology placed spirituality at a distance, making it always suspect to guardians of orthodoxy.[7]

The human wisdom of literary criticism helped Christians understand aspects of Bible reading which they had not perceived before. Study of biblical texts as texts, as well as being the Word of God, brought new light to Bible reading. Fear of emptying the text of the element of the Word of God led to the reaction of fundamentalism which does not want to go beyond 'What the Bible says'. This exclusive role given to the literal meaning of the Bible can cause problems of interpretation when texts written in one ancient cultural setting are used as a guide to living in a totally different time and culture. Fundamentalism is one attempt to hold on to something solid when the sands of time seem to be shifting.

Specialized knowledge of the ancient languages in which the Bible was written helped to produce a verbal exegesis which reinforced insistence on the literal meaning of texts. This verbal exegesis dominated the field of biblical studies until recently. Now the insistence is on the hermeneutical problem of reading an ancient text in a different situation. Hermeneutics, which is one of the keys to theological reflection at present, recognizes the need for rereadings of Scripture, patristic texts and liturgical symbols in the light of historical and cultural change. Time wreaks its ravages even on the apparently most eternal of formulations:

> Even symbolism, then, does not necessarily escape the ravages of time. Even though in the majority of cases biblical symbols still strike responsive chords because of their archetypal or primordial character, it cannot be assumed that they will function 'timelessly' in the sense of requiring no hermeneutical explanation or translation.[8]

Words – even God's Word – imply recipients who are people contemporary with its reading or proclamation.

The conviction that God still speaks and that the Holy Spirit, sent by Jesus from the Father, is to bring to our mind all that Jesus has said – not as dead letter, but as living light for today – makes Christians search the Scriptures to find God's Word for them in new situations. It is not a question of finding ready-made answers in the Bible for problems undreamt of when it was written, but of seeing the way God acts so as to discern where the Spirit is leading the Church and the world in our time. The analogy with the Word of God addressed to his people in particular circumstances in biblical times provides a clue as to the direction God's ways are taking today. The central Old Testament event of the Exodus, liberating an enslaved people to serve God in freedom and create a history that would be salvific for many, is reflected on today by peoples and groups suffering various forms of slavery and discrimination. Addressing the biblical account with new questions brings to light aspects of the ancient text which had not been adverted to before.

The aim of contemporary Bible-readers, in the liberation theology tradition, is to find the way to act in their concrete situation. This directly ethical and action-oriented aim is found to suit the biblical narrative which tells the story of the vicissitudes of a people in its historical journey, now near, now further from God. The right way to act so as to accompany the breathing of the Spirit ('orthopraxis') is the aim. The biblical hermeneutic for this is found in the 'see, judge, act' method.

Theologically untutored people, listening to the voice of the Spirit, learn to discern in the Bible enough gleams of light to advance in the way of the Kingdom. Without faith in the action of the Spirit it would be impossible to be so sure-footed on this pilgrimage or to have the courage to create their own piece of history. The model of the Exodus, meditated on to see how God acts in history, gives the courage to see themselves as children of the Father and God's people destined for freedom and not slavery. Structural analysis of the contemporary situation allows this sort of exegesis, placing in a social and historical context what might have been examined only in the categories of individual morality. The wisdom of the human sciences – in much the same way as Greek philosophy did before – contributes to the reading of the Bible and allows its message to be deciphered in a new context. Sociology and economics helped the Theology of Liberation; Black and Feminist Theology used history, while cultural anthropology is now enlisted in the struggle.

In Catholic countries in Europe the Bible had been written off as irrelevant to contemporary concerns because it was seen as having been wrong on so many issues decided by science. This perception of the Bible (according to Jean Daniélou) contributed to the distancing of the working class from the Church. With Vatican II, the Bible regained a fuller place in Catholic theology and was made available to ordinary people. In Latin America, the Bible is becoming once again the property of the community – as it was at the time it was compiled. It is being read by communities of the poor who hear it speaking of them and to them, in a way which is Good News. The Bible is the great source-book for liberation and, once more as in early centuries, it has to be hidden under the floor of poor people's huts when soldiers search for 'subversive literature'. The Word of God is alive and speaks to slaves of liberation: it is no wonder that possession of a Bible can mean an arbitrary sentence of immediate death. Jesus Christ, condemned for his message of Good News to the poor, is heard by the poor loud and clear today. This rereading in the context of their own lives unites communities of the oppressed to his Mystery. Community members are willing to risk torture and death for a Bible many of them cannot even read.

Contemporary hermeneutics insists that every reading of a text is a rereading. Every time a person reads a text he or she brings to it a new awareness, fruit of accumulated experience, and this new viewpoint prompts the reader to ask new questions of the text, questions which it had not occurred to him or her to ask before. The text, being looked at from a new point of view, yields up new insights. Women today who are aware of the degree of discrimination to which their sex was victim in patriarchal cultures will try to read between the lines of a biblical text in order to see what it would have said had the writer been a woman with feminist awareness. Those who are suffering apartheid look to see what the Bible has to say about the equality of races before God. Those who are exploited economically look for clues as to how Jesus treated the poor, or search in the Prophets for God's attitude to the dispossessed of the earth.

It is in the Word of God, first of all, that light is sought to illuminate the search for the way forward in new situations which challenge the lives of Christians. New problems arising suggest new questions to be asked of the sources of faith, and the new light obtained in the search reveals hitherto undiscovered facets of the one Mystery of Christ. Those who search find the Mystery to have been active all along in places they never thought to look. Pastoral agents, men or women versed in biblical lore, play a mystagogic role in helping communities of the poor find guidance in the Word of God for their journey towards liberation from political and economic exploitation. Only when the question has been asked of the Bible does it become clear that thousands of years before Karl Marx used the language of 'oppressor and oppressed', the prophets of Israel had denounced similar situations in similar language (Amos 4:1; Micah 2:1–2), and the divine threats of vengeance against political or economic oppressors of the poor could not be bettered by any violent revolutionary, whose threats of vengeance are limited by historical time.

When basic ecclesial communities of the poor discover in the Bible God's preferential love for them in Christ and their closeness to the cross of Christ in their sufferings, their lives are changed. They find that they can be sharers in the Paschal Mystery through their being unjustly exploited, despised and brought to early death, and gain hope from the victory of Christ. For people long used to having a low opinion of their own worth, the discovery that they are really children of God, made in his image, is productive of a rich spirituality which inspires them to struggle to recover the image in which they were created. The struggle for liberation comes to form part of the conversion process by which they pass from a situation of dumb acceptance of their inferiority as a fatality, or even a curse from God, to a realization that their vocation as children of God, fundamentally equal to any of their human brothers and sisters, demands that they assert that equality and recover that divine image of which they have been despoiled.

The human reality adopted as vehicle for God's revelation in the Old Testament was that of a people, as in the New it was that of Christ. A people is a social entity, organized politically and socially – and in olden times always religiously as well; it has its own history in a sense that no individual has. The Old Testament narration of the vicissitudes of the Israelites in living out their vocation as God's people gives grounds for a people today to see the political, social, cultural and economic conditions of their life as integral to their vocation as Christians. They feel themselves to be heirs, in some sort, to Israel of old, through their faith.

For the oppressed of today's world, because of this social character of Old Testament revelation, the struggle to change unjust structures of a society which keeps them in thrall to a tiny minority of powerful and wealthy men and women can become part of their growth as Christians and of their living out of the Mystery of Christ. Before their conversion to the God whom they found to be their caring Father, rather than Patriarch turning a blind eye to their sufferings, they found it less painful to bow their heads under the lash than rise up against those who were systematically destroying the image of God in them. Imitating the individualism of their oppressors, each one had tried to make what deal he or she could with the owner of their body and soul. It was in the common faith of their community that they found the solidarity necessary to undertake the struggle to change the situation of their lives. In the struggle they found themselves and discovered the nobility of their enterprise. Even when political victories proved few and far between, the constant reflection in faith on their real situation revealed so many gifts of leadership and wisdom in the group that this newfound source of personal and communal empowering welded them together and assured the adherence of each.

The one Mystery of God, initially revealed to Israel of old in the Exodus and given completion in Christ's Passover, is lived by communities of the poor and despised who learn to discern in their lives the Word addressed to them today. The pedagogy which they employ in their Bible reading is mystagogic; it leads them into the heart of the Mystery through the privileged path of God's Word.

NOTES

1   M. L. Cook, 'Revelation as metaphoric process', *TS* 47 (1986), p. 392; cf. also N. Frye, *The Great Code* (New York; Harcourt Brace Jovanovich, 1983), pp. 5ff.

2   H. Riley, *Christian Initiation: A Comparative Study of the Interpretations of the Baptismal Liturgy in the Mystagogical Writings of Cyril of Jerusalem, John Chrysostom, Theodore of Mopsuestia and Ambrose of Milan* (Washington: Catholic University of America Press, 1974), p. 139.

3   E. Mazza, *Mystagogy* (New York: Pueblo, 1989), p.13, explains the purpose of this type of allegorizing in terms of mystagogic theology, though he admits that exaggeration in the use of allegory gave mystagogy a bad name: 'Allegory has historically been the death of mystagogy.'

4   The primary biblical passage is Genesis 1:26–27 with 9:6; the archetype according to which man was created is Jesus Christ (Col 1:15ff.; and re-created: Col 3:10).

5   B. Bobrinskoy, 'Mystagogie trinitaire des sacrements' in A. M. Triacca and A. Pistoia (eds), *Mystagogie: Pensée liturgique d'aujourd'hui et liturgie ancienne* (Rome: Edizioni Liturgiche, 1993), p. 30.

6   H. Riley, *Christian Initiation*, pp. 140–1.

7   St John of the Cross was not the only creative spiritual person to fall foul of the Inquisition; his mysticism seemed dangerous – now he is a Doctor of the Church.

8   A. C. Thiselton, 'Hermeneutics and theology: the legitimacy and necessity of hermeneutics' in Donald K. McKim (ed.), *A Guide to Contemporary Hermeneutics* (Grand Rapids: Eerdmans, 1986), p. 155.

5

MYSTAGOGY AND LITURGY

Liturgy is the original home of mystagogy. Mystagogy had its origins in liturgy and spent the patristic centuries in close association with it, placing its indelible mark on the lenten season and liturgy of initiation. For several centuries – the formative centuries of the Church – there were no schools in our modern sense (in Alexandria one was opened for catechumens), and there was no written educational material. The liturgical assembly on the Lord's Day was the weekly occasion for those already baptized to deepen their experience of the Paschal Mystery. Participation in the lenten, mystagogical celebration of initiation of new members was an annual occasion for remembering and deepening the original commitment of the whole community. The liturgy itself had sufficient mystagogic capacity to prepare generations for martyrdom.

The normal development in the evolution from an oral to a literate culture is marked by a diversification of elements: work and leisure, education and cult, therapy and religion separate into autonomous departments of life. The move into cities accentuates this specialization. To have a form of mystagogy which is not part and parcel of regular liturgical celebrations belongs to this process; Rahner's intuition went in this direction and must be declared legitimate. What would be dangerous would be to have mystagogy forget its roots in liturgy. Developments such as that beginning with Maximus the Confessor, and that associated with the name of Karl Rahner, may not be pronounced unhealthy. What would be unhealthy is if one of these newer applications of the practice were to pretend to a monopoly on mystagogy, or forget to return, for orientation, to the sources of Christian mystagogy, whenever a new sense of direction is called for.

The charismatic movement renews the experience of the presence and action of the Holy Spirit in the common prayer and in the daily living of Christians. Our liturgy, even since Vatican II, has been so centrally controlled and so intellectualized that the spontaneity aimed at by the charismatic renewal is virtually impossible in the setting of the liturgy. Separated from the liturgy, which was their cradle in New Testament times, charismatic experiences, for all their validity, tend to the eccentric, the individualistic or the trivial. True spirituality ought to strive for and tend towards that unifying of Christian life which is one of the definitions of mysticism. This should include the unifying rather than the splintering of liturgy and other Christian experiences.[1] The profit to Christians would be great if the free and spontaneous prayer and experience of the Spirit, common in the charismatic movement, were to be allied once more to Catholic liturgy, as they were in New Testament times.

The Second Vatican Council admits that the liturgy does not exhaust the Church's activity. It does state clearly, though, that it is from the liturgy that all the Church's activity draws its strength. When speaking of private prayer and devotion the liturgy document of Vatican II makes it clear that the centre and purpose of such devotions is to have the core of the Paschal Mystery become the centre of the life of the Christian; 'always being given up to death for Jesus' sake, so that the life of Jesus may be manifested in our mortal flesh' (2 Cor 4:11).

The liturgy document of Vatican II, which was the best prepared of all the original texts, and the first document approved by the Council, set the scene, if not the agenda, for the Council as a whole. Its vision of the Church, drawn from the oldest and most constant liturgical tradition, influenced the document on the Church. It was impossible, of course, that the later perspectives of the Council, notably those contained in the Pastoral Constitution on the Church in the Modern World, should have influenced the document on the liturgy. And this means that there is a lack of overall balance in the Council documents if they are simply read each one as it stands and in separation from the others. A work of comparing, contrasting and harmonizing the earlier documents in the light of the later ones is needed if the Council is to be understood, even in the historical setting in which it was celebrated. To produce its fruit today, the developments following on the new perspectives opened up by *Gaudium et Spes* must constantly impregnate pastoral-liturgical research and advance.

The rereading of the Liturgy Constitution in the light of the ecclesiology and 'this-world relatedness' of the later conciliar texts, especially *Gaudium et Spes*, is a work which still largely remains to be done. One of the reasons that liturgical renewal has slowed down – almost to a standstill – in recent decades is that it has not integrated into its vision of liturgy the pastoral perspectives of that last great document of the Council. An example of this is the strangeness with which Rahner's project of a mystagogy for men and women living their lives in the world of today comes across. The perspectives of the Church in the world of today have not been assimilated into our liturgical consciousness.[2]

A hermeneutic for modern liturgy must begin from contemporary situations which call for incorporation into liturgical celebration. The starting-point cannot be uniquely the past or it is there that we will remain. It is from the standpoint of pastoral situations and needs today that the usefulness of ancient forms and language must be judged, unless we are to remain in museums. There is a place for historical studies but there is also a place for pastoral applications – and it is the latter which are urgently required at present – if even the utility of the former is to be saved.

The reintroduction of the older, patristical and liturgical understanding of 'Mystery' has influenced all theology since Vatican II. The 'Mystery of Christ' is what the Council called a Christocentric theology with emphasis on salvation history. This Mystery of Christ in the history of salvation, leading to the construction of God's Kingdom, allows the sacraments to be seen as actions which place the faithful in the transforming current of that salvific history. The sacraments are directed towards a deepening of Christian life in the Spirit. The Eucharist, as the privileged celebration of Christ's saving deeds, is not only a way to personal communion with God in Christ, but also a pledge to work for the coming of the Kingdom inaugurated by his resurrection.

The Orthodox liturgy and theology do not make as sharp a distinction between what is sacramental and what is not as do the liturgy and theology of the West. The Word of God, icons, funeral rites and the Church itself are seen as sacramental – times and places in which the grace of God is operative. In this view, the basic function of all sacramental rites (mysteries) is mystagogic, to initiate us into the Mystery of Salvation.[3]

Liturgy is meant to reach the Christian people of God in each generation. To do this, the symbolism on which it lives must become relevant and audible to them. The interests and concerns of contemporary humanity must become starting-point for prayer and symbols which reach out to the Mystery in the heart of the world, making it transparent to those who have good will and are in search of God. Each component of liturgy must be pressed into service in this mystagogic task. Poetry, homiletics, music, dance, architecture, sculpture, mosaic, painting, vestments, furniture, light and sound equipment . . . must be used to lead into experience of the Mystery. This experience is needed, not in any superficial and theatrical sense – all too tempting in some milieux – but with the sobriety of the Roman tradition and the objectivity of sound theology, while taking full account of the local culture. For too long we have insisted on 'raising the people up to the liturgy'; as though there existed some liturgy outside of place and time and independent of the cultural language which it uses. We have attempted to impose a uniform super-culture as coming from the Spirit, in contrast to the incarnation by which the Son of God came among us, human like us in all things but sin (Heb 4:15). The role of the Holy Spirit, in the incarnation and always, is to make material things transparent to the divine, and pliable before God's action; not at all to operate outside of and above things human. For those who have faith, the things of this world, especially the human, are transparent to mystery.

Every liturgical act and object is mystagogic, each in its own special way. The mystagogic character of liturgical music, for example, has recently been well expressed in a document, *Universa Laus*, emanating from the international group of that same name: the role of music in liturgy goes well beyond the scope of what is verifiable. As is the case with all symbolic signs, music points to something beyond itself. Music opens up an unlimited field of meaning which it awakens, and free reactions which it provokes. For the believer music becomes sacramental and 'mysterion' of the realities celebrated.

Two poles of concern meet in the employment of art in liturgy: that of 'beauty' and that of the holiness of the action whose aim is to be prayerful and 'sacred'. These two must be balanced so as to have a music (or other art form) that harmonizes the values of the celebrating congregation with a celebration in spirit and in truth. Sacred music aims at revealing and realizing the human being made new in the risen Christ. The music must allow the believers to cry the *Kyrie eleison* of the oppressed and the *Alleluia* of those risen with Christ, while it sustains the *Maranatha* of hope in the coming of the Kingdom.

The Apostle Paul invites the Colossians to let the word of Christ dwell in them richly as they sing psalms and hymns and spiritual songs (*ōdais pneumatikais*, Col 3:16, which some take to be 'charismatic' 'singing in the Spirit'). There is evidence, in the commentaries of Augustine on the Psalms, that the 'Alleluia' in the eucharistic celebration was at that time a 'charismatic' example of a community 'singing in tongues'.[4] Augustine's remark, *qui bene cantat, bis orat*, is well known and implies that song adds to the prayerfulness of prayer.

The chant of the Church, which arose from the synagogue singing of psalms, gradually developed into the Gregorian chant, so much praised for its ability to express depths of meaning in the texts being sung, and mentioned with approval at Vatican II. The original placing of the *schola cantorum* (readily visible in the oldest examples of 'basilica' extant in Rome) was in the centre of the church building, between clergy and the rest of the faithful and between the 'ambones' from which readings or solo chants were executed. This position of the *schola cantorum* expressed architecturally the organic closeness of chant to sacred text and action. The baroque displacing of the choir to an organ loft over the entrance-door is all too symbolic, as J. A. Jungmann liked to point out, of the new place of music in liturgy – half-way between the Church and the world. It was the age of symphony orchestras playing Masses by Beethoven or Mozart, sung by multi-voice choirs, 'with liturgical accompaniment at the altar'.

The innate tendency of any of the arts employed in liturgy is, as Jungmann again points out, to express itself unrestrictedly, to the detriment of the whole. The mystagogical potential of the arts in liturgy must be brought to act through the co-ordination and co-operation of all concerned. The overall mystagogic aim must never be forgotten. This means that the planning of the place and carrying out of liturgy in its ensemble may not be handed over to the exclusive execution of the exponent of any one art: those who have pastoral responsibility for the liturgy may not abdicate that responsibility, but should maintain constant dialogue with the specialists who participate in bringing the arts to the service of the overall mystagogic task. The former should prepare themselves to exercise that overall co-ordinating function.

Architecture is another vehicle with special mystagogic potential. The architecture of churches, and their fitting and furnishing, express what the building symbolizes for Christians. Unlike the temples of some religions, the Christian church building is not thought of as the shrine where our God dwells; instead, it is primarily the place for the community of the people of God to meet for worship – especially for the Eucharist – and for whatever else clearly expresses the true and full identity of that people. This theology has roots in Judaism, whose *qāhāl* or assembly of God's people was forerunner of the Christian *ekklēsia*.[5] For the Christian the church building is an expression of the Church-Assembly. It is because the assembly is God's house that the building is that too. Paul reminds the Christians that (collectively) they themselves constitute the temple of God (1 Cor 3:16) and make up a building raised on the foundations of the apostles and prophets (Eph 2:19f.).

The dignity of the individual Christian as temple of the Holy Spirit derives from the prior ecclesial fact that all together form, as a community, the temple of God. In 1 Peter (2:4f.), the Christians are likened to stones to be used in the constructing of a building which has Jesus Christ for cornerstone, once rejected, but now become base of a new social edifice. In relation to the church building, mystagogy consists in having Church members grow in consciousness of their identity as a community devoted to the transformation of this world into God's Kingdom; such identity should be symbolized in this social and historical church building, its architectural form and the use to which it is put.

Dance does not form part of Roman liturgy at present. Yet, in other religions, dance is a mystagogic factor of prime importance. Inculturation in

Africa or Asia, whose traditions integrate dance into so many aspects of life, may yet bring dance to Christian liturgy in a role not unlike that which it has in the initiation rites of those oral cultures.[6] In the Hindu tradition, the spiritual and mystagogic role of dance is outstanding.

Martyrdom is another way to approach the Mystery of Christ's death and resurrection. From the *arcosolio* of the catacombs, to the *martyria* built over the tombs of the apostles and other martyrs, on through the circular shrines and relics in every altar, the cult of the martyrs has been a constant in Christian history. Not until the feast of St Martin of Tours (d. 397) did a saint, not a martyr, have a celebration in the Christian Church, and then it was because his way of life was deemed to have constituted a witness resembling that of martyrdom.[7] The proximity to Christ's passion of those men and women who shed their blood for the Kingdom, in witness to the Gospel, made their lives dear to the first Christians. Also, of course, persecution was an ever present possibility during those centuries and the example of fidelity given by the martyrs 'in spite of dungeon, fire and sword' was a powerful encouragement to others who were at risk.

In Latin America, today, where Christians once more face the powerful of this world in the name of Gospel values, martyrdom is frequent. Because it is mostly the small people, leaders of local communities or young lawyers devoted to helping the dispossessed gain what is their legal right, who suffer, these martyrs go unsung in the wider Church. Only when violent death touches a bishop, like Romero, who took up the cause of the poor, does it make headlines. It requires faith and a commitment approaching that of the persecuted to appreciate the evangelical character of their struggle. That sort of faith mostly remains hidden.

As it was in the infant Church, the death of the otherwise undistinguished, duly celebrated in small communities faced with the same threats and temptations, is motive for joy and for courage to face the same end with Christ if necessary.

Cult is so often, and so easily becomes, ideological – an integral part of the national *status quo*, affirming it and legitimizing it. Camus's remark often rings true, 'Christianity, historically, has pushed the remedy for evil beyond the bounds of history . . . We are told to wait, and, during this time the innocent continue to die.' If the situation legitimized by liturgy is evil then the liturgy becomes a party to scandal. In the context of basic ecclesial communities, which live in a world and culture geared to the prosperity of the powerful at the expense of the poor, what has liturgy done to change things? Liberation *in* liturgy is not enough – freedom in matters of vestment, furnishings, language or song – liberation *through* the liturgy is needed.

In this context of liberation through liturgy, the annual celebration of the Israelitic Passover – celebration of political and religious liberation – is paradigmatic. The reason for the Exodus was liturgical: 'Thus says the Lord, the God of Israel, "Let my people go, that they may hold a feast to me in the wilderness"' (Exodus 5:1).[8] The annual celebration of the Pasch reinforced the unity of the people and confirmed them in their vocation as people of God. Pagan religion attempted to influence the divinity through ritual cult alone; biblical revelation insisted on the inseparable link between cult and justice, between the offering of sacrifice and respect for the rights of the poor (Amos 5). The Exodus was a splendid example of an event harmonizing cult and justice on a predominantly religious note.

In the New Testament and whole Christian tradition, there is no doubt but that the centre of Christian cult lies in the Paschal Mystery of Jesus – his death and resurrection. The Old Testament roots of the Pasch ought to make it clear that the historical and social elements of the Mystery still belong to it. Unfortunately, even in the renewed liturgy after Vatican II, the insertion into history of Catholic liturgy has not always been visible.

Once the Latin American Church began to place itself at the service of the transformation of the continent, which it saw as full of injustice and misery, that Church could no longer continue to celebrate the liturgy as before. Liturgy, too, must work towards the liberation from sin in history. The Medellín Conference of the Latin-American Episcopate (1968) speaks of the Exodus and Passover: the passage from inhuman to more human conditions of life is seen as a passover from death to life in Christ. This intuition situates the work of development, as later that of liberation, in the dynamic of the Paschal Mystery.

The liturgy of basic communities frequently recalls the salvific interventions of God in history; not just in the past history of his people, but in history here and now. It recalls liberating events that those present have seen and their action helped bring about: installation of a water supply, better public transport, land for planting crops, houses built by teamwork, and so on. The active presence of God in these events, through which his people pass over from death to life in becoming free from slavery, is seen and celebrated by the community. Christ's Easter is continued in that of his people, and the final, eschatological resurrection is anticipated in these liberations in history.

Celebrations spring up everywhere that basic communities meet: in houses, under a tree, in a public square, under a bridge. The necessity of celebrating without a priest – or remaining without any liturgy – leads to a facility in celebrating the Word of God in various circumstances. It also leads to smaller and more intimate celebrations where everyone knows the others by name and informal conversation is not outlawed; where the sharing of each one's understanding of the Scripture readings is simple; where the Prayers of the Faithful are often long laments about each one's life and their common condition. Frequently there is a collection of money, clothes or food for those still more poor;[9] people's lives, as seen by themselves, become matter for celebration.

The celebration, in turn, brings the participants' lives into direct contact with their faith – bridging that gap between faith and life which is so much regretted in the Churches of the industrialized world. The communities overcome the gap between faith and life by overcoming that between people and rite. Such unity in the celebration makes the in-built mystagogic character of liturgy more effective.

In basic communities, liturgical ministries or services are usually carried out by a team, collegially. Sometimes even the presidency is shared: one doing the introduction and prayers, another co-ordinating the readings and sharing which follows, while communion may be distributed by a third who is minister of the Eucharist.

Liturgy is made up of signs and symbols. In Latin America, it should be celebrated with signs adequate to express the present struggle of the people for liberation: chants, prayers and other elements drawn from the culture of the people. Post-Vatican II liturgical renewal has so far been done from the top down, ignoring the cultures of areas like Latin America and Africa.

In spite of some appearance of lack of creativity in the liturgy of basic communities, there are important gains. Community participation in liturgy is occurring on a large scale after a long liturgical winter. The official rite is still so centred on the priest that absence of a priest allows the community to appear as liturgical actor for the first time in centuries. The lack of ordained ministers has led to a multiplicity of ministries and services – impossible during the centuries of presbyteral monopoly of ministries in the Western Church. The distance which has long separated a clericalized priesthood from the people is being attenuated through emphasis on the community. It is possible that when the ministerial crisis in small communities all over the world is resolved, it will be in the direction of finding ministers in and for each community, rather than subordinating community to ministry as at present.

In the eschatological liturgy of the Apocalypse, the people who had suffered and been martyred, but now carried palms in their hands, sing and adore the Lamb. The Lamb which was slain stands victorious by the throne of God, liberator of his people. This victory is celebrated in basic communities, not simply in the inner recesses of individual hearts, but in the external forms of a community liturgy of God's people; it is a celebration of an eschatological victory, though realized by people still living in misery; it is a liturgy which is opposed to all the celebrations of the Beast and death, which seek to do away with the life of the poor. This is a liberational liturgy.

All true liturgy is mystagogic, because it leads the people – initiates them – into the heart of the Christian Mystery. Liturgy leads the people through three phases: sacramental remembrance of the saving event of Christ's death and resurrection (faith); celebration of the unifying presence of Christ's love, operative in the community now (charity); and celebration – by anticipation – of the final victory of the Lamb and of those whom he has freed from sin and death (hope). As it unfolds in history, the Mystery embraces all of time, past, present and future: 'Jesus Christ, yesterday and today, the beginning and the end, Alpha and Omega; all time belongs to him, and all the ages . . .'[10]

Rites, liturgical gestures and actions, are mystagogic. These too follow the culture of an age so that they may speak the more clearly to the experience of participants. Many early Christian rites and gestures were inherited from Judaism, whereas later times inculturated buildings, decoration, garments and gestures from the surrounding civilization. The Middle Ages – less well known – used symbols from Germanic culture: hands clasped by the hands of the feudal lord, hands joined in prayer, 'tools' of office presented during ordination, and others. These rites helped lead the participants through the everyday realities of their culture to the Mystery of Christ and his Kingdom. The challenge to liturgists and to communities of the faithful today is to find symbols which speak to contemporary culture and local needs.

The skeleton liturgy issued from the post-Vatican II reform was intended to be just that – a common skeleton whose flesh and blood were to be provided from local cultures. In our world-Church, in a pluricultural world, now more evidently so than at the time of the Council, the challenges of inculturation are more than academic. Islam, for example, will sweep over the rest of Africa if the Christian Churches do not learn to inculturate to a degree approaching that achieved by the children of the Prophet. A conviction of superiority, invisible, doctrinal or historical, must prove itself by translation into the cultural language of those it hopes to incorporate. Mystagogy, being based on experience, if not inculturated, is inoperative.

The Easter Liturgy is so mystagogic that, at times, the Mystery becomes almost palpable. The sober symbolism of the ancient Roman rite, as retained for the Easter Vigil, with emphasis on the basic human symbols of fire, light and water, is ultimately more powerful than the emotional, Germanic (in Jungmann's reading of it) symbolism of the Good Friday liturgy. Candle and font express anthropological understandings of faith and new birth.

The font as womb parallels the Mother Church symbol and brings echoes of the Earth Mother of old. Recent interest in ancient gods and myths recalls that the 'principalities and powers' were not annihilated (it is not the Creator's way to annihilate) but brought into submission to the risen Christ who sits at the right hand of the Father, 'far above all rule and authority and power and dominion, and above every name that is named, not only in this age but also in that which is to come' (Eph 1:20–21). 'He disarmed the principalities and powers and made a public example of them, triumphing over them in him

(Christ)' (Col 2:15). Its agricultural origins were caught up into the Jewish Passover. Christ's Paschal Mystery celebrates, in its fullness, the Pasch and all lesser cults, with the positive aspirations of the powers and myths attached to them.

Baptism is one of the great themes of the Easter Vigil. Paul sees it as inserting the Christian directly into the heart of the Mystery which is so close on that night:

> Do you not know that all of us who have been baptized into Christ Jesus were baptized into his death? We were buried therefore with him by baptism into death, so that as Christ was raised from the dead by the glory of the Father, we too might walk in newness of life.
>
> For if we have been united with him in a death like his, we shall certainly be united with him in a resurrection like his. (Rom 6:3–5)

Current emphasis on work for the coming of the Kingdom of God sees everything which promotes life as contributing to that coming and everything which favours death as inimical to it. Symbols of new life and of life-enhancing action are not difficult to find. Clean water, flowers, green leaves, work and struggle for better living conditions for the exploited . . . Symbols of death are all too prevalent and may serve to be rejected ritually, much as catechumens of earlier times blew (or spat?) in the face of the Devil during the Renunciation which preceded the act of commitment to Christ.

NOTES

1   Cf. B. Secondin, *I nuovi protagonisti, movimenti, associazioni, gruppi nella Chiesa* (Turin: Edizioni Paoline, 1991), pp. 38, 86–9, 89–92.

2   The whole issue of *Concilium* vol. 2, no. 7 (1971) is devoted to this problem, as the Editorial makes clear (pp. 7–12). Herman Schmidt, one of the editors, then provides an acute examination of the problem, 'Liturgy and modern society – analysis of the current situation' (pp. 14–29); J. Llopis, 'The Liturgy celebrates God's presence in the world and his invitation to man' (pp. 121–30), makes some attempt to spell out this perspective. In the same issue of *Concilium*, Cornelius Dippel also raises the problem, 'Liturgy in the world of the sciences, technology and commerce' (pp. 98–108), but does not offer concrete solutions.

3   B. Bobrinskoy, 'Mystagogie trinitaire des sacrements' in A. M. Triacca and A. Pistoia (eds), *Mystagogie: Pensée liturgique d'aujourd'hui et liturgie ancienne* (Rome: Edizioni Liturgiche, 1993), p. 27; an example of the mystagogic outlook of Oriental liturgy is J. Corbon, *Liturgie de source* (Paris: Cerf, 1980).

4   Cf. E. Wellesz, *A History of Byzantine Music and Hymnography* (Oxford: Clarendon, 1961), p. 41, note 1: Augustine, *Enarr. in Ps. xcix.* 4, PL 37, col. 1272:

> Qui iubilat, non verba dicit, sed sonus quidam est laetitiae sine verbis: vox est enim animi diffusi laetitia, quantum potest exprimentis affectum, non sensum

comprehendentis. Gaudens homo in exsultatione sua ex verbis quibusdam, quae non possunt dici et intelligi, *erumpit in vocem quandam exsultationis sine verbis*; ita ut appareat, eum ipsa voce gaudere quidem, sed quasi repletum nimio gaudio, non posse verbis explicare quod gaudet. (Italics mine.)

5 L. Bouyer, *Life and Liturgy* (London: Sheed & Ward, 1955), chapter 3.

6 The Instruction on the Inculturation of the Liturgy, published on 25 January 1994, on the eve of the Synod for Africa, by the Congregation for Divine Worship, opens the door in no. 42 to liturgical dance in the Roman rite.

7 To this day, the Antiphon for the Magnificat for the Second Vespers of the feast of St Martin (11 November) shows the need felt to justify celebrating someone who was not martyred: 'His holy soul, though spared the sword of persecution, was not deprived of the martyr's palm.'

8 Gustavo Gutiérrez, treating of the Exodus in his book *We Drink from Our Own Wells* (London: SCM, 1984), does not at all consider that this wish to go out into the desert in order to celebrate the feast of Yahweh was a legal ruse to enable the Israelite slaves to escape from Egypt. He takes it as the genuine *raison d'être* of the whole enterprise – an interesting difference between exegesis done from the standpoint of an enslaved people, and that done in academic isolation from such conflict.

9 Poverty in Brazil reaches scandalous proportions, considering the overall wealth of the country: a 1993 World Bank report shows that, in Brazil 44 per cent of the population lives below the poverty line. The average for Latin America is 31.5 per cent, Brazil dragging down the overall average. The figure for Mexico is 11 per cent and for Peru 9 per cent.

10 Easter Vigil of the Roman Liturgy, quoting the Apocalypse (1:8, 17), a theme which is taken up again in the last two chapters as though to bracket the whole book.

6

MYSTAGOGY AND COMMUNITY

Recent groups and movements in the Church which seek to provide religious formation for the baptized in the modern city provide a strong base of relationship in which the evangelizing process can take place. There is an absolute need of a sense of belonging for real maturing in faith – for real maturing of any sort. An old adage holds that to live alone one must be either saint or devil; most of us are neither and so we need fellowship. In any case, no one ever reached sanctity except through an initial experience of faith lived in common. If some few men and women manage to go on to live an eremitical life after many years of Christian community living, they are exceptions and rare fruits of maturity gained through living in the midst of others. It is likely that had Rahner's intuition as to a mystagogy for men and women of the modern world found expression in an organized movement, providing support, it would have flourished instead of remaining without visible fruit. The companionship of fellows of like persuasion is necessary for the growth of any ideal.

Not a closely-knit community, but a network of diverse social relations, typifies modern urban living. In some sense, the city as a whole constitutes a natural community; it is so thought of for infrastructure, politics, football and sundry other activities. Citizens live in one part of the city, work in another and pursue their leisure-time activities in another: different aspects of urban socializing occur in different groups. To attempt to make people live all aspects of their lives in the one grouping or 'community' is to do violence to the nature of urban man and woman – to limit the freedom of choice that is their urban birthright. This poses a problem for the ecclesiality of Christian living in a modern setting. Early attempts at building basic ecclesial communities came up against rural prejudices: clergy (mostly of rural origin) found it hard to credit that the anonymity of urban living could be other than pagan, that not to know the name of the people living in the next house or apartment could be humanly normal. Also, it seemed incomprehensible that only those marginalized, through poverty, from the mobility and freedom of choice proper to the city, could form real communities in which many aspects of life were shared.

Prior to urbanization, narrowly sociable rural society was the norm. Families in rural areas were thrown together inescapably. If a family got on well with neighbours life-long friendships developed. If deep differences led to rifts, life-long and even centuries-long feuding might result. Indifference was impossible. This is a fact of rural life. Many pastoral agents still believe the rural pattern of relationships to be somehow more godly than the more complex network of urban relationships. The rural origin of so many clergy and religious certainly contributes to this prejudice. Community strictly so called – living many aspects of life with the same persons – is characteristic of rural areas or of non-urbanized peripheries of cities. More rarely is it found in 'urban villages', where rural patterns of dwelling and employment persist as islands in a metropolis.

Some of the best reflections, to date, on the situation of the Church as community in modern urban centres, are to be found in the work by Joseph Comblin, *Théologie de la Ville*, published in 1968.[1] Comblin insists on the need for the local Church – the diocese, or Church of the bishop – to take over from the territorial parish as basic pastoral structure for planning and organization in the city. Because urban man and woman do not live many social aspects of their lives in the same grouping of persons, the Church in the city must discover new forms of community: some sort of network of institutions, movements, groups allowing the urban Christian to find conditions for growth in faith.

The city itself, as organic and complex whole, constitutes a natural community. Salvation must be worked out inside the structures of the modern city itself, by transforming them, and not by taking flight from the city. Urbanized men and women live the diverse facets of their existence as Christians in a number of different groupings: family life, work, political involvement, exercise of a conversion apostolate, and so on. Whatever its shape, community is required for mystagogy. A Christian identity cannot be achieved or developed without the collaboration of others.

Modern groups and movements provide a sense of belonging that confers a clear identity affecting the whole outlook of members. The group may meet formally at relatively long intervals, but its ethos, and the initiation which confers it, overflow into other areas of life. Because the group has Catholic affiliation, it can make membership in the larger Church community come alive. All this forms part of the mystagogic process of initiation into the Church as *locus* for explicit living of the Mystery of Christ.

It is through different experiences that mature self-awareness arises. The interpretation of experience comes through the community to which the individual belongs – 'community' here being used of the cultural unit. That community has an important role to play in the initiation of the individual; it continues to have a decisive role in the interpretation of all experience for each member of the community:

> The community provides the overall horizon of understanding within which human experience begins to make sense . . . The self develops out of experiences with reality, especially the reality of the human community composed of other selves.[2]

The role of the local community in Bible reading is coming to be seen as vital. Reflection on biblical hermeneutic tells us that it is the community which, out of its own current experience and life situation, reads the Bible in such a way as to draw from it the nourishment it needs at the moment. New aspects of the one Mystery of Christ are highlighted when the community's current experience of God active in the world is compared with the experiences of the Judeo-Christian community across the centuries, as found in Scripture and the lore of the Church. The community is not an inert spectator during Bible reading; it is an active participant bringing its own experience and questions to the Word of God. As Christian experience over the ages affirms and charismatic renewal groups bear out today, the Spirit is more readily available to the community than to the individual. In fact, some exegetes maintain that the true 'spiritual sense' of Scripture is that arrived at by a community reflecting on the Word of God in openness to the Spirit, today. It is the Spirit, and not some rule of thumb, which allows the community to discern its way forward through reflection on God's action in history – a reflection which allows the community to discover how to act so as to direct its own history toward God.

Initiation implies entry into the ecclesial community; but in recent times it has most often been considered from the point of view of the individual who becomes a Christian, or of the individual who is discovering a deeper Christian identification with Christ. The present, industrialized world quest for a human initiation into adult living tends to be coloured by the individualist culture of those places in which it is pursued. Traditional societies always saw initiation as an affair of the whole community. The viewpoint of the individual is a dangerous one from which to begin a consideration of any aspect of Christian belonging, because it falsifies the approach through making all initiation into Christian life a matter of the conversion of individuals.

The progressive 'taking over' by the Spirit, in the life of the Christian, is one of the definitions of a 'mystical life'. The community aspect of this taking over by the Spirit is outlined in Vatican II and enshrined in the liturgy: it is the whole Church which must undergo a maturing of faith and become more docile to the action of the Spirit of Christ. The transformative role of Christ's followers begins at home: it is the Church, *semper reformanda*, constantly renewing itself, which is first to be transformed. In Old Testament times, the prophets of Israel called the attention of the people and their rulers to the need for conversion in order to continue faithful to the Exodus and Alliance in changing political and cultural situations. In our day, prophetic voices in the Church, calling attention to misuse of power, over-attachment to outworn pastoral practices, or to the need for greater flexibility in the exercise of the Church's mission, fulfil a similar mystagogic function. Such prophetic interventions help guide the Church beyond facile continuity, to where the Spirit appears to be beckoning today. The prophetic ministry may be seen as mystagogic, in the sense that it deals with new experiences and with the need for change in order to respond positively to them. A positive response to a new challenge reveals hitherto undisclosed riches of the Mystery and produces new ways of working for the coming of the Kingdom. Teaching in predominantly doctrinal and intellectual terms does not easily get in touch with experience. The ecclesial perspective is not easily captured in any spirituality which is centred on the experience of the individual.

In its luminous fourth paragraph, *Lumen Gentium* describes the process of sanctification of the Church by the Holy Spirit: sent at Pentecost, the Spirit is to continually make the Church holy, giving believers access through Christ to the Father. The life-giving Spirit is that 'fountain of water springing up to eternal life', through which the Father gives life to sinful humans, until he raises up their mortal bodies in Christ. The Spirit dwells in the Church and in the hearts of the faithful, as in a temple, praying in them and bearing witness that they are children of God. The Spirit leads the Church into all truth . . . rejuvenates and renews it constantly through the power of the Gospel: conducting it to perfect union with its Spouse.

Here the Spirit is seen as inspiring a mystagogy of the Church as a whole – as a community and not just as composed of individuals. The entire Church is to be led to the Father, and to final, perfect participation in the Mystery of Christ's resurrection. It is the whole Church that is kept young in the Spirit. It is the Church that is Bride of Christ. The Spirit and the Church long for and look forward to the Coming of Christ, the Spouse. This final perspective is the correct one: it is Christ's Second Coming – and not the death of the individual – that is the crowning event in salvation history. The future event of the parousia belongs to the Mystery of Christ and constitutes the perfecting of his Kingdom. It is lived in hope by the Church as part of its identity in the Spirit, figuring explicitly in every Eucharist as integral to the celebration. 'The Spirit and the Bride, say (to the Lord Jesus), "Come"' (Apoc 22:17).

The final phase of the Mystery, to be celebrated in the full flowering of the Kingdom, at Christ's return, has been consistently overlooked in the centuries marked by individualist philosophy. Even earlier, overemphasis on the frightening aspects of the Coming of Christ (' . . . men fainting with fear and with foreboding of what is coming on the world; for the powers of the heavens will be shaken', Luke 21:26), to the exclusion of the joyful realization of the promise of full salvation ('. . . look up and raise your heads, because your redemption is drawing near', Luke 21:28), dissuaded many from devotion to so horrific a prospect. The eschatological dimension of the New Testament was lost in the hellenization of the Christian message and has not yet been recovered by the mainline Christian Churches.

The Second Coming is made less attractive through its espousal by fundamentalists and alternative Churches whose 'spiritualizing' places eschatology outside of history; while progressive theologies fear that emphasis given to the final coming of Christ will take from the struggle for transformation of this world, pushing 'salvation' back once more into a future and 'spiritual' domain. The solution is to give positive emphasis to the Second Coming, integrating it into a complete view of eschatology. This view is a fully historical and ecclesial one. The Christian community, and not the individual, is primary – it alone merits the designation of Body of Christ. The individual is saved in Christ and, as part of his Body, enters into the heavenly places in him:

> But God, who is rich in mercy, out of the great love with which he loved us, even when we were dead through our trespasses, made us alive together with Christ (by grace you have been saved), and raised us up with him, and made us sit with him in the heavenly places in Christ Jesus.[3]

The degree to which so many of the baptized see their future in terms of each one's death reveals the extent to which a less than Christian understanding of death, centred on the individual rather than on Christ, has taken over from the New Testament perspective. It is the coming of Christ which constitutes the future for the Christian: an historical, communitarian and social event, in which the death of the individual finds its fuller meaning. Mystagogy has a major challenge ahead of it to lead Christian people to an appreciation of this vital future event in the Mystery of Christ. A better understanding of Christian hope, through which the future of the Mystery is already celebrated, is overdue. Hope is not a pallid 'it would be nice if . . .', but is centred on the solidity of our looking forward (*firmitas expectationis*) to the future event which has as guarantee Christ's ascension to the right hand of the Father. The Ascension – another forgotten facet of the Mystery – is the Feast of Christian hope.[4]

Christian liturgy has always had a threefold reference: to the past, remembered (in the Scripture readings); to the present union of all in the love of Christ, celebrated sacramentally and enhanced in the celebrating; and to the future, when what is now celebrated in hope will become reality. This last and oft forgotten facet of liturgy does not in any way exclude work for the coming of the Kingdom through the transformation of this world – its structures as well as its men and women. The liturgical celebration, which should be based on the real life experience of the community, equips those celebrating to go forth and put into practice what they have contemplated. The Mystery of Christ's death and resurrection is always pointed towards the Kingdom for whose proclamation Jesus came and to whose construction he dedicated himself unto death. The hope now celebrated in community will find its realization in community too, the community of the whole Christ, come in glory.

The Apocalypse, last book of the Bible, is generally considered to have been written to give comfort to Christians in crisis, chiefly that of persecution. The Roman Empire is under judgement and will be totally destroyed – its evil is such as to render it irreformable. What is said in allegorical but decipherable terms of Rome is applicable also to other empires and regimes throughout history. That the Apocalypse describes the final victory in terms of a city gives the lie to the idea that the future will be in terms unrelated to this world. Nor will the sacred and holy be limited to the temple; the whole city will take on characteristics which are specific to temples now:

> And the city has no need of sun or moon to shine upon it, for the glory of God is its light, and its lamp is the Lamb. By its light shall the nations walk; and the kings of the earth shall bring their glory into it . . . (Apoc 21:23–24)

The historical, communitarian vision of the Apocalypse – which derives its unity from the central figure of Christ, the Lamb who was slain but now reigns gloriously – places the Christian future squarely in terms of Christ and his community the Church, to which the nations have now been added.

The liturgy of the mysteries was the context which produced the word 'mystagogy', and even if new shades of meaning may legitimately be given the term, its liturgical origins must never be lost to sight. The liturgical community was the context in which Christian mystagogy came into being. The mystagogy developed by the Fathers – Cyril of Jerusalem, Ambrose,

John Chrysostom and Theodore of Mopsuestia – had its setting in the local Church gathered for Easter worship. Theodore, for example, explaining the 'Epiclesis over the people', applies the mystical understanding of eucharistic unity to the neophytes:

> *The bishop also prays that the grace of the Holy Spirit may come upon all the assembly.* The new birth has made them into a single body; now they are to be firmly established in the one body by sharing the body of our Lord, and form a single unity in harmony, peace and good works. Thus we shall look upon God with a pure heart; we shall not incur punishment by communicating in the Holy Spirit when we are divided in our views, inclined to arguments, quarrels, envy and jealousy, and contemptuous of virtue. By our harmony, peace and good works, and by the purity of heart with which our soul looks upon God, we shall show that we are waiting to receive the Holy Spirit. In this way, by communion in the blessed mysteries, we shall be united among ourselves and joined to Christ our Lord, whose body we believe ourselves to be, and through whom we 'become partakers of the divine nature'.[5]

Mystagogy concerns the whole Church: in the liturgy it is lived by the local community along with the catechumens and neophytes; and the whole local Church grows and matures together with the new members.[6] Pastorally sensitive Christians perceive the vital role to be played by community if the Church as instituted by Christ is to be truly alive. This was the intuition governing the efforts of pioneering pastors in France immediately after World War II, who perceived that their country had become a mission land. They saw the uselessness of individual conversions, especially among the poorer classes with their in-built class solidarity, if there were not a real community in which their new-found faith could grow, meet support and begin to produce gifts of leadership.

This community dimension raises a major problem about giving the name mystagogy to individual spiritual direction. It is true that all genuine spiritual direction, while immediately concerning the individual, always seeks to have that person – even if a hermit – become part of the ecclesial community. Too often this insertion was at an invisible and 'spiritual' level which failed to provide the qualities of mutual support and sense of identity which ordinary mortals require for Christian living. Mystagogy traditionally has a direct community reference, being itself celebrated in and by a community – a concrete group of men and women which provides interpersonal relations and in which ideals are shared. That it may provide a real religious experience it is necessary that the community be a real one. This is one of the points at which the original liturgical shape of Christian mystagogy – and indeed of mystagogy in traditional religions – ought still to have some value as norm. Spiritual orientation for the individual member, or couple, as part of the group dynamic of certain movements and groups, might merit the label mystagogic; spiritual direction of the individual, not so easily.

The revived *Ordo* (RCIA) has insisted on the role of the community in the initiation of adults today; it sees mystagogy as built on a twofold experience: the neophytes experience the celebration of the sacraments of initiation, and they experience the Christian community: 'The distinctive spirit and power of the period of postbaptismal . . . mystagogy derive from the new, personal experience of the sacraments and of the community . . .'[7]

The community or ecclesial dimension of the Christian in the world of today is a complex one. Rahner, when he proposes a new style of mystagogy, emphasizes the problem of discovering the Mystery in the changed circumstances of the life of modern, middle-class, urban dwellers in the First World (Germany). He saw that the crisis which led to the search for such a new mystagogy was bound up with the need for *aggiornamento* or renewal in the Church, a Church which was failing to provide pastoral care relevant to the needs of contemporary men and women.

More than twenty years ago, the theologian Yves Congar confessed that in his celebrated book on laity in the Church, he had got his correlatives wrong: in the book which he had published in the 1950s he had contrasted 'laity' with 'clergy'. Now he saw that the correct binomial expression was 'community' and 'ministry'.[8] The question is not one of having enough clergy to look after the laity, but how living Christian communities may have the forms of ministry which allow them to grow and the ministers required to service that growth. Today this is seen as including the question of having communities sufficiently alive to produce the ministers they require. This is not simply reducible to statistics about 'vocations', or to the search for candidates for clerical seminaries.

In Latin America, the new form of Christian community-living, called Basic Ecclesial Community (CEB), has grown up over the last quarter century. It is seen as a new way of being Church. A new way through being a very old way, although it has original features. The old element is that of 'ecclesiogenesis', or the way in which the Church grows. Our clerical era, now with us for so many centuries that some think it traditional, saw the ministers of the Church as above and somehow outside the people. Church growth – missionary work is a good example of this – consisted in sending ministers who exercised their ministry in some place and gathered a congregation for worship, preaching, baptizing and organizing works of charity. After some time – several centuries in many places – they thought about providing local ministers and started 'seminaries'. The new Christians had not been considered mature enough to be ministers before.[9] The prevailing hierarchical model of Church allowed missionaries to think that, having imported generation after generation of priests and bishops, they had established a Church. In a Church which sees itself as People of God, this is not possible for long. Ministry is seen as something developing inside the People of God, as part of its organic structuring. Ministers are seen as coming from the community rather than as being brought to it from outside. It is no longer possible to imagine that one has a Church if there is no organically structured people of God present. Missionaries are certainly still necessary, but the importation of ministers from outside, for the day-to-day running of the Church, cannot now be seen as valid, even for one generation. A mature, living community – like any living organism – is capable of reproducing itself. If it does not produce the ministers necessary for its own maintenance and missionary work, it is sick, and any ministerial structure which relies on such importation is in dubious health. To wish to keep communities in tutelage, as too immature to produce responsible ministers, is paternalistic.

In practice, a community of the baptized, gathered to reflect and pray about the problems which beset their lives and to celebrate their common faith in Jesus Christ whose victory gives them hope, soon produces ministers. Within a few months, members of the community begin to discover charisms and put them at the service of the whole. There is an abundant supply of vocations in most communities; they must be allowed to blossom. In Brazil, thousands of Pentecostal and other Protestant communities have, in this generation, ministers who were baptized into the Catholic Church. We must ask whether, during their Catholic years, they had not got a vocation to ministry, a vocation they were not allowed to exercise.[10] In vain do we pray to the Holy Spirit for 'vocations', if we insist on pre-determining the only kind of reply we will accept, when the New Testament leaves us free.

True mystagogy, leading the baptized into an ever deeper experience of the community dimension of the Mystery of Christ, cannot be divorced from the charisms which make their appearance in the community. The community's freedom to give itself the ministerial structure it needs and is capable of providing – within the overall structuring of the Church – must be respected. Communities are interdependent and the collegiality of pastors is to serve this intercommunion of the Churches. Hence the primacy of charity: if the love of Christ is not experienced in relations with those who are at the service of unity and creativity, other aspects of the ministry are exercised largely in vain.

Evidently, spontaneous generation of living communities does not happen; someone has to animate communities of the baptized, or evangelize those of non-Christian religions. It does not have to be our present style of ordained ministers who do either of these tasks. Laity may preach the Word. Historically, the example and daily proximity of lay Christians has accounted for the vast majority of conversions in areas of the world new to the Church.

Ordained ministers are not always needed for the animating of communities. A problem arises when a community wishes to celebrate the Eucharist and has to call on the services of a presbyter from outside to preside over the celebration. Each week at present, tens of millions of fervent members of living communities are denied their Catholic right of celebrating the Lord's Supper on the Lord's Day. This, not because their communities are lacking in vitality, but because recent cultural modes of ministry, which have nothing to do with the Lord's command, are the only style allowed in the Roman communion. Ironically, every Sunday tens of thousands of communities, in every continent, that want to be Catholic are deprived of *the* liturgical badge of Catholic belonging – the Mass. And why? Not for any theological impossibility, but for pastoral reasons that become steadily less convincing. Has the Church reached the point of pastoral inability to give itself the forms of ministry it needs to ensure its vitality and growth?

If the poor are to come to exercise a decisive influence on the history of the Latin American Continent, it will be necessary to let them have their own space in the Church: a space with due autonomy. The alternative is a Pentecostalist takeover. The poor will become spectators as a neo-conservative Church goes its way (as happened in the past) without them; the difference being that this time they will be outside the Church.

Without due ministry, the community becomes structurally deficient and truncated. What is the ecclesial position of 'Catholic' communities which, through no fault of their own, have to live for decades without regularly celebrating the Lord's Supper on the Lord's Day – more often than not without even being able to celebrate the Easter Vigil? Is the Mystery of Christ adequately visible in such communities, and if not, why not? Were anyone to preach or teach this sort of community as an ideal, he or she would immediately be condemned as heretical.

Criticisms of basic communities sound hollow when such communities, anxious for the integrity of Catholic life, are deprived of it for reasons which are far removed from the New Testament models of community. The theological ban on the ordination of women is based on more flimsy arguments than those that would press the Church to adopt ministerial structures permitting a large and growing portion of the Catholic flock weekly access to the Eucharist. If, in decades to come, small communities have grown so used to non-eucharistic celebrations that they are no longer interested in having a Sunday Eucharist, who will be to blame? Not the simple faithful.

It is true that many small communities are too much under clerical control to develop their own liturgy for celebrations of the Word. Ironically, true liturgical renewal will most likely come from those groups that – for lack of an ordained minister – are free to make the community, and not the minister, the centre of their celebrations. In such situations, new-style ministers to preside at the Eucharist, when eventually they are permitted, will exercise only one of a plurality of diversified ministries. When there are no priests left to monopolize all ministries in the community, we may see the emergence of a more balanced ministerial structure. In this new beginning, the community and its concerns will be prime material to be 'read' and celebrated in the light of the Mystery of Christ.

Throughout history, it has often been persecution that forced the demise of obsolete ways and inspired pastoral creativity. Today, it is cultural change that leads to the demise of obsolete forms of ministry. It is official slowness to adopt new forms that forces the people of God to become creative and bring about renewal that they hoped for in vain from the top. Erosion of the credibility of pastors is an inevitable result of this tardiness.

One of the problems faced by those who initiate the individual baptized into Christian living is the absence of living communities in which the now fervent may regularly live and celebrate their newfound faith. So many of the modern Church 'movements', which employ brilliant dynamics in the initiation of new members, are not (as basic communities aspire to be) 'the Church at the local base'. They cannot, therefore, provide an ongoing community where the members may regularly live the faith they have rediscovered. Not being a 'Church' the movement does not seek to provide sacramental celebration, nor normal community belonging. Members only frequent meetings of the movement for special activities. Their conversion has not been lived in the context of an organic community of which they were or became part.

The Christian community is part of the Mystery. There is no leading of candidates into the Mystery without their becoming, through the same process, members of a particular community. Initiation into the one is inseparable from membership of the other.

NOTES

1 J. Comblin, *Théologie de la Ville* (Paris: Presses Universitaires de France, 1968).
2 D. Lane, *The Experience of God: An Invitation to do Theology* (Dublin: Veritas, 1981), p. 10.
3 Ephesians 2:4–6. This passage is part of the development of the theme which forms the second reading for the liturgy of the Ascension (Eph 1:17–23). The Ascension is the feast of Christian hope. That hope is based on the fact that Christ our Head has already gone before as guarantee that his Body will follow.
4 The average Catholic, in many lands, knows the feast of the Assumption much

better than the Ascension. This is not to deny to the popular conviction the possibility of having intuitively captured a feminine aspect of the mystery of the divine not adequately catered for in current theology.

5   Theodore of Mopsuestia, *Baptismal Homily* 5, 13: E. Yarnold, *The Awe-Inspiring Rites of Initiation* (Slough: St Paul, 1972), pp. 246–7. Yarnold points out in a footnote (to p. 247) that: 'There is such a close connection between the presence of Christ and of the Holy Spirit that communion can be described as "communicating in the Holy Spirit".'

6   No. 4 of RCIA sees the role of the entire Christian community as central; it even makes the community of the faithful the 'first minister' of Christian initiation.

7   RCIA 39–40.

8   Y.-M. Congar, *Ministères et communion ecclésiale* (Paris: Cerf, 1971).

9   There is an African country where, after more than five centuries of Christian presence, over 80 per cent of the clergy are still imported.

10   Cf. J. Comblin, 'Questões a partir da prática das CEBs no Nordeste', *REB* 50 (1990), pp. 335–81.

7

MYSTAGOGY AND MYSTERY

Mystagogy means initiation into an experience of the mystery. What do we mean by mystery? The Greek 'mysteries' were secret rites, which might be revealed only to the *mystai* or initiated. Secrecy was observed about the rites to avoid profanation through frivolity or imitations (Christians later adopted a rule of silence about their rites for similar motives, the *disciplina arcani*). The Greek mysteries were normally presided over by a hierophant and the candidates were initiated by a *mystagōgos*. Underlying the rites was a myth, but this was only rarely expressed in words, and while the great issues of human freedom and afterlife were debated, the mystery religions never developed a full theology – unlike Christianity.

In the Christian borrowing of the term, the initiation is into an experience of the Mystery of Christ. The Greek word *mystērion* and its equivalents in other languages, and the notions which lie behind them, are, therefore, key concepts and expressions in dealing with the theology of mystagogy. The early history of the expression 'mystery' coincides with that of 'mystagogy'.

When translating into Greek, the Septuagint Old Testament does not use the word *mystērion* for the Hebrew word *sôd* (secret). *Mystērion* only appears in those books which achieved their definitive form in the Hellenistic period. The notion of 'mystery' as a secret is found in the Old Testament. The Hebrew word *sôd* appears to have originally meant a council and then the results of the deliberations of the council, or *secret counsel*: there was a Jewish belief that there was a heavenly council which decided about things human. The true prophets were those who had been made privy to the heavenly counsels and thus had a special vision of things. Mysteries were also symbolic visions of the future. In the book of that name, Wisdom is initiated into the knowledge of God.[1]

The Old Testament, notably Deuteronomy, presents Moses as fulfilling a function that would later be considered as mystagogic. He explained the meaning of the Exodus to those who had come up with him out of Egypt, sometimes being accompanied in the explanation by the elders of the people. In the Book of Deuteronomy his explanations become more pointed as they progress (Deut 29:2; also 1:1; 27:1). To listen to the 'Ten Words' of the Law and put them into practice was a mystagogy giving entry into knowledge of God and allowing every believer to become a prophet as Moses had wished.[2]

False prophets led the people into false understanding of the mystery of God. Jeremiah reminded the greedy king Shallum that his deeds showed him to be short on knowledge of God. In Scripture, knowledge of God and of the mystery of his ways are linked; God's ways always include concern for the defenceless:

> Did not your father eat and drink and do justice and righteousness?
> Then it was well with him. He judged the cause of the poor and
> needy; then it was well. Is this not to know me? says the Lord.
> But you have eyes and heart only for your dishonest gain, for
> shedding innocent blood, and for practising oppression and violence.
> (Jer 22:15–17)

The Torah (book of the Law) was more than a book of morality, it was a liturgy celebrating the presence of God, a mystagogy leading from knowledge of the Law to appreciation of the mystery of divine Wisdom. Wisdom, given in the Spirit, makes people friends of God and prophets. The experience of their unmerited sufferings led the innocent, and the humiliations which they had undergone led the Chosen People, to pass from knowledge of the Law to some understanding of the mystery of divine Wisdom.[3]

The relationship between the Old and New Testaments is seen most clearly in the fact that the Paschal events of Christ's death and resurrection were accomplished in the setting of the Paschal feast: the Last Supper being the Paschal Meal in memory of liberation from slavery in Egypt. Any correct mystagogy of the Eucharist must take into account this central fact. The Eucharist was instituted on the night when Israel was doing what Moses had commanded in memory of God's hitherto greatest intervention in the history of his people. This far-from-coincidental date gives mystagogic illumination to Jesus' words, 'Do this in memory of me', Jesus now becoming the focus of memory and promise. Over the centuries, much hermeneutical ink might have been spared had this relationship between the central event of each Testament been kept in mind; the Church's liturgy (*lex orandi*) once more proving a guide to faith and theology (*lex credendi*). Liturgical celebration of Easter includes celebration of fundamental elements of this created universe, fire, light, wax and water. The spring setting of Easter in the northern hemisphere (something may have to be done about this now that the majority of Catholics live in the southern hemisphere), reminds us of the agricultural setting of the origins of the feast. Some scholars have thought that it was reflection on the Exodus event which led the Israelite theologians to conclude that it must be this same Yahweh who created the world, and that it was the Exodus revelation of Yahweh which led to the Genesis understanding of creation.

Sunday is the original feastday (*primordialis dies festus*), through a tradition deriving from the day of Jesus' resurrection. The faithful gather on that 'eighth day' to celebrate and keep in mind the Paschal Mystery of Jesus through listening to the Word of God and taking part in the Eucharist.[4] The whole structure of the Church's year is also intended to highlight the central position of the Paschal Mystery.[5]

The Mystery was lived by Jesus so totally that he *is* the Mystery. He is also the witness to the Mystery and the one who proclaimed the Mystery in words. 'I must preach the good news of the kingdom of God to the other cities also; for I was sent for this purpose' (Luke 4:43). Jesus first preached to the crowds, but when they rejected him and their leaders began to plot his death he began to go about in more restricted circles and concentrated more on the formation of the disciples. Also, Jesus' activity of initiating others into the saving mystery of his Kingdom changed course when his message was rejected and his historical career, instead of passing through joyful acceptance, passed through death and resurrection, his work for the Kingdom leading to his death.

The formation given by Jesus to his disciples was *the* true mystagogy, but it was never called that in the Bible. We do not concentrate on it here because we are concerned with a particular concept 'mystagogy' and with the terms that historically accompany and express that concept or have affinity with it.

The Synoptic Gospels use the word *mystērion* of the Kingdom of God (the Kingdom of Heaven in Matthew) in reference to Jesus' explanation of the parable of the sower: where Jesus tells the disciples that to them it is given to understand the mystery of the Kingdom (Mark 4:11; Matt 13:11; Luke 8:10). Jesus' mission is defined and understood in terms of the Kingdom of God. His original mission in history was the proclamation of that Kingdom. The price that Jesus paid for the proclamation and founding of the Kingdom was his death – a source of consolation to others who are threatened with death for the sake of their proclamation of that same Kingdom. The resurrection was a striking vindication of Jesus' work, and ushered in the new time, that of the Church and of the building of the Kingdom, which Jesus will bring to its plenitude at his Second Coming.

Paul and John stress the theological understanding of Jesus' mission, rather than its historical unfolding (which is presented in the Synoptics), and consequently give pride of place to the Paschal Mystery, rather than to the Kingdom. A total view of Jesus' mission includes the founding and development of God's Kingdom and the Easter Mystery of Jesus' death and resurrection that set the seal on the founding of that Kingdom. Some recent theologians would add the baptism of Jesus, establishing his identity as Son of the Father, filled with God's Spirit as he began his mission by proclaiming the coming of the Kingdom.[6] When we speak of the Mystery of Christ, or of the centre of our faith, both Kingdom and Easter event must be included. It is part of the challenge of liturgy today to include the perspective of God's Kingdom in the eucharistic and other celebrations which can easily remain individualistic and disincarnate if they are interpreted only in terms of a narrow and ahistorical understanding of the Paschal Mystery.

Justice is not done to the New Testament sources when an understanding of the Mystery of Christ in terms of Jesus' death and resurrection is presented as theological, while an understanding in terms of the Kingdom of God is seen as merely historical. The theology of the one Mystery of Christ may not separate Jesus' work for the Kingdom from the Paschal event of his death and resurrection. The resurrection was a turning point in the progress of the Kingdom; after his resurrection Jesus could maintain that all power was given to him in heaven and on earth (Matt 28:18). He had come into possession of a kingdom far greater than any promised by the Devil in the temptation at the outset of Jesus' career; he had become *Kyrios*, Lord of the entire cosmos.[7] It is not as though Jesus' interest in the coming kingdom ceased when rejection by his people led to a change of route and into the way of suffering and death. In the first chapter of Colossians the Father is seen as rescuing the Colossians from the powers of darkness and bringing them safely into the kingdom of his Son, by whom they are set free. In being raised from the dead Jesus comes to have first place in all things.[8]

Paul is minister of the Gospel, to preach the mystery once hidden but now made manifest; the mystery is Christ in the 'saints' (those who believe in Christ), the 'hope of glory'. It is Paul's aim, through his preaching, to have every one 'mature in Christ' – the aim of all Christian initiation and mystagogy. This Christian maturity will allow the Colossians to judge accurately of new situations, and even more, to discern what is obsolete in old religious practices (Col 2). If the mystery and the Christian's part in it are duly understood, then the moral consequences will be clear. Paul is not a moralizer insisting on correct conduct not based on anything deeper; he knows that initiation into 'belonging to Christ' is the only way to true and efficacious morality: the mystery is Christ in us – from that all else derives.

How superior is this view of Christian life to that so often propounded in a style of 'religious education' in which a multitude of precepts and abundant moralizing are detached from their root and source in Christ: the Mystery is fragmented into pieces, each of which is called a mystery; morality is made 'scientific' and detached from mysticism and people wonder how faith got separated from life! Later in that letter, Paul uses the term 'Mystery of Christ' as expressing the centre and sum of his preaching – sufficiently challenging to the powers that be to have landed him in prison:

> Pray for us also, that God may open to us a door for the word, to declare the mystery of Christ, on account of which I am in prison, that I may make it clear, as I ought to speak. (Col 4:3–4)

Mystagogic emphasis on the one Mystery as centre of all: worship, evangelization, catechesis, morality and mysticism, is the key to Christian formation which is in such disarray at present, often trying to fill up through intellectual indoctrinating the lack of a central religious experience.

Luke shows Jesus still speaking about the Kingdom after his resurrection (Acts 1:3), and has two angels tell the disciples to stop looking into the clouds and instead to keep their feet on the ground as they prepare the Second Coming (Acts 1:10–11). With Jesus' ascension began the time of the Church which lives in hope, anchored to him through the veil (Heb 6:19–20), but working for the spread of the Kingdom (Acts 1:7–8). Enthroned now at the right hand of the Father (Luke 22:69), Jesus, nevertheless, remains with his own (Matt 28:20). He will come again, and that coming will make visible to everyone the exaltation of Jesus – the poor, rejected and marginalized One – and bring the Kingdom to completion.

In the Apocalypse, *mystērion* is used in a sense very close to that employed in the Old Testament apocalyptic literature: for the elucidating of the secrets of the divine designs – seen only in prophetic vision until the end of time – when they will be rendered evident in judgement.

The use which Paul makes of the expression 'mystery' initially links it to divine wisdom as well as to apocalyptic expectation. In 1 Corinthians 2:7 Paul speaks of 'a hidden wisdom of God in a mystery, a wisdom which God predetermined before the ages for our glory, which no one of the rulers of this world had known'. The emphasis is on the wisdom of God which shows up the shallowness of human knowledge. Throughout his letters there is a gradual development and clarification of the notion of mystery.

In Romans, Paul begins to equate the mystery with Christ. In the Epistles of the captivity, in Colossians and in Ephesians, this identifying of the mystery with Christ becomes usual; in Colossians the doctrinal focus is christological, in Ephesians, ecclesiological.[9] In the letter to the Ephesians, the notion of mystery finds its fullest development: the revelation of the mystery is made in Jesus, in whom all things are to be united. Paul prays that the believers at Ephesus may receive a spirit of wisdom and come to know the workings of God's power in them in association with the raising of Jesus from the dead and his glorification as head of all things. The mystery involves a revelation made by the Spirit and requiring wisdom and insight, but the mystery is also effective in bringing about a new situation of salvation:

> When you read this you can perceive my insight into the mystery of Christ, which was not made known to the sons of men in other generations as it has now been revealed to his holy apostles and prophets by the Spirit; that is, how the Gentiles are fellow heirs, members of the same body, and partakers of the promise in Christ Jesus through the gospel.[10]

Before the fourth century, the Fathers are cautious in their use of the word *mystērion*. At the turn of the third century, for Christian sacred rites Tertullian prefers the Latin word *sacramentum*, an expression referring to the military oath and a sign, but which had connotations of both secrecy and initiation; he was still wary of the language of the pagan mysteries. It is only when the young Church had reached a certain degree of organization, growth and institutionalization that the moment had come to borrow the term 'mystery' from other (traditional) religions. For Ambrose, *mystery* referred to the event in salvation history, called 'mystery' by Paul; *sacramentum* referred to the rite which made the saving power of this event present to those celebrating it in faith.[11] It was in this way that our current word 'sacrament' emerged.

In the Bible, 'mystery' is not a concept but a reality, an event in the history of God's dealings with the world. It was the theology which developed under the influence of Greek philosophy that led to thinking of mysteries as concepts – truths to be believed – rather than the reality prior to and underlying any belief in or articulation of it. Also, the events presented in the Bible are closely connected so that the Old Testament is built around the Exodus/Alliance axis and that is intimately related to its fuller flowering in Christ's Passover from death to life, his primary work for the coming of God's Kingdom. The Mystery as revealed in Scripture has an organic unity. The development of facets of that mystery, first by liturgy and then by theology, easily forgot the unity and tended to make each facet a 'truth' in its own right. Later still, refinements on the theory of faith made of these truths equal objects of faith, so that their hierarchical ordering and organic interrelation were forgotten.

Killian McDonnell contrasts the way in which catechetics looks at the Mystery with that which is typical of mystagogy. The contrast arises in a commentary in which he compares Cyril of Jerusalem's catecheses with his mystagogies. McDonnell begins with the quotation from Cyril's first mystagogical homily, 'seeing is far more persuasive than hearing':

> Experience precedes explanation. Mystagogy, not didactic instruc-
> tions (catechesis), surrenders the ultimate reasons. From outside the
> mystery the teacher marks the road through knowledge to experience.
> From inside the mystery the mystagogue leads the way through
> memory to insight. The bishop/mystagogue takes the neophytes
> on a journey into the centre of the remembered experience . . .[12]

It is quite a different thing to describe the Mystery from the outside through the use of theological categories and to experience the Mystery from the inside through initiation.

The history of the expression 'mystery' in Catholic theology, from the fourth century until the middle of the nineteenth, includes a progressive intellectualizing of what started out as something to be experienced or at least to be proclaimed in kerygma. Already in the Alexandrian theology, the tendency was under way and *mystērion* began to be used for dogma, whereas Paul had never separated it from the kerygma or proclamation of the central Gospel message – the Mystery of Christ who is Lord and King through his death and resurrection and is proclaimed as such, the proclamation itself being a saving event.[13] This separation of dogma from the proclamation of the Mystery is only part of a larger rift, between theology and spirituality, later aggravated by the intellectual brilliance of the Scholastics, and intensified in the nineteenth century struggle against rationalism. In Origen's time (the third century), spirituality, exegesis and theological speculation were still united, but, soon afterwards, due to controversy against heretics, and helped by the influence of Roman law with its precision and definitions, theology became centred, not on the biblical Word of God, but on 'doctrines'.[14]

From the end of the adult catechumenate in the Latin liturgy (in the sixth century), until recent times, sacramental catechesis tended to become, more and more, the 'learning' of doctrine: an intellectual procedure which paralleled the growing predominance of the dogmatic in the field of theology. As faith was thought of as an assent to truths, doctrine was all-important. Theology became arid and generally unpreachable; devotion and popular piety became mostly untheological. From early on – the eighth to ninth centuries – unscriptural, and sometimes fantastic, allegorizing gained a great place in preaching and popular piety. During those centuries, from patristic times until our own, the notion of mystagogy or experiential initiation into *mysteries* was neglected.[15]

The theological controversies, from the fourth century onwards, led gradually to changes, not only in theology, but also in preaching, in liturgy and in the devotional outlook of the faithful. The anti-Arian struggle led to emphasis on the divinity of Christ, with consequent diminution of his humanity and its mediation. This, in turn, opened the way for devotion to the Blessed Virgin Mary as human mediator between humanity and God: the figure of Christ had become so remote that a human representative of the interests of humanity was sought – this, of course, in balanced theology, is Christ's role. The changes wrought by the gradual conversion of the Germanic peoples of northern Europe added an element of subjectivism and personal approach to religion, very different from the measure and objectivity characteristic of the Roman style.

From his vantage point as a historian of liturgy and catechesis and of the theological thinking underlying changes in each, J. A. Jungmann has written of the anti-Arian struggle in the Germanic lands. He says that the 500 years from the end of the patristic era to the beginnings of Scholasticism saw an unprecedented change in religious thinking and in the religious institutions which flow from such thinking. It was at this time that, in the Gallican lands, Epiphany and Christmas began to take over from the Easter Feast as centre of Christian devotion and celebration. Celebration of the Trinity takes over from the paschal understanding of Sunday.[16] The sweep of salvation history as represented in art gives way, in the ninth and tenth centuries, to concentration on individual historical details; the Christ in Glory of the apses of the basilicas gives way to scenes from the life of Christ, and to the crucifix. The crucifix, which has become symbol of Catholic Christianity, is a late development and a partial symbol. The older and more traditional symbol united death and resurrection in a representation of the cross which saw it bathed in the glory of the resurrection. This more complete understanding of the Paschal Mystery is represented in the Celtic crosses and in the crosses in use in the Ethiopian Church to this day. Western Catholic liturgy conserves in its rubrics one aspect of an earlier understanding which venerates the wood of the 'cross' on Good Friday (*ecce lignum crucis*), without any attempt to superimpose on it an image of Christ.

It was the romantic Germanic mentality, according to Jungmann, that placed one-sided emphasis on the suffering Christ while forgetting the resurrection. This mentality can be seen at work in the naming of the chief basilica in Jerusalem: in early times the whole church was called the Anastasis, from the resurrection, whereas since the Crusades the edifice which arose over the same spot has been called the Church of the Holy Sepulchre. The same building (or its successor on the same site) changes its name according as life or death is the facet of the mystery stressed. In other churches, the Judgement replaces the *majestas Domini*. In piety an analogous change takes place: in antiquity, it was the mystery which predominated; in the Middle Ages, it is human effort, moral action, which matters; the subjective and individual are emphasized. It is interesting to see these anthropological characteristics, usually associated with the 'modern', already identified so early in European history.

Related to these developments is the rise of medieval 'mystery plays'. These grew out of the liturgical Sequences, and specifically out of the *Victimae paschali laudes* of the Easter Eucharist. Freely composed verses in the vernacular were intercalated between the Latin strophes which already had a dialogue structure. The reading by different people seems to have gradually given rise to dramatization (that is, to the assumption of roles by actors who pretend to be other than themselves), and finally to the writing of new texts. From these plays grew our modern theatre.[17] These plays took three different shapes:

(a) Mystery plays that followed the liturgical cycle and were initially in Latin;

(b) Miracle plays representing the lives of saints;

(c) Morality plays that employed dramatized personifications of virtues and vices.

Here the *Pater* and *Credo*, traditional catechetic and mystagogic material, were dramatized.[18] Some of these plays were produced by the medieval trade guilds. It is interesting to note that it was glosses on the 'Sequence' for the central feast of Easter that gave rise to the Mystery plays, which later followed the division into a multitude of 'mysteries' largely unrelated to the Paschal Mystery.

In 1959, shortly before Vatican II, Karl Rahner criticized the notion of mystery then current in theology, and which had, at that time, been inherited especially from the First Vatican Council in its struggle with rationalism.[19] The definition of *mysterium* formulated by Vatican I in answer to the errors of the semirationalists defined 'mystery' in a technical intellectualist sense. In this Scholastic sense, mysteries are truths to which the assent of faith is given. The reality or object to which the statement refers is also the mystery and this is not denied; but it is the *truths* which are commonly called mysteries and not the realities of which they speak.

Rahner's critique helped towards the demise of a highly intellectualist notion of 'mystery'. He urged a more total, experience-based understanding of mystery that would refer to the object expressed by statements of truth rather than having 'mystery' consist in the statements about those objects.

In his view of mystery, Rahner is heir to the theological rather than the liturgical tradition. The liturgy sees and celebrates the Mystery as primarily the Mystery of Christ in his death, resurrection, ascension (and Second Coming). For Rahner, 'The trinitarian mystery of God' is fundamental, while he admits that 'The mysteries of soteriology can undoubtedly be reduced to the mystery of the Incarnation'.[20] It is the incarnation and not the Paschal event that he singles out. He does insist that the mystery of the Trinity is related to our salvation and is revealed only on this account, but he does not take the liturgical view that it is the salvific mystery, in the biblical foreground, that is *the* Christian Mystery. He also insists that every facet of Christian life must be related to the Trinity, this 'primordial mystery of Christianity'.[21]

Rahner attempts to include the dimension of experience in the notion of mystery; he says that:

> When entering upon the doctrine of the Trinity, we need not hesitate
> to appeal to our own experience of Jesus and his Spirit in us as given
> in the history of salvation and faith. For here the immanent Trinity
> itself *is* already present. The Trinity is not merely a reality to be
> expressed in purely doctrinal terms: it takes place within us, and
> does not first reach us in the form of statements communicated by
> revelation.[22]

To accept, as central to their faith, the affirmation that God became man – body and soul – the Greek Fathers had to undergo an intellectual conversion which involved changing their Greek philosophical ideas about the superiority of the spirit over everything material. Accepting in faith the centrality of Jesus Christ did not necessarily mean being able happily to incorporate the reality of the incarnation into their theology. Origen seems to have held that the image of God in the human was limited to the soul, and some see his struggle in favour of a spiritual sense of Scripture as bound up with this Greek notion. Augustine had convictions very close to this and his influence on theology, throughout the Middle Ages, was enormous. In the background of Greek thinking always lurks the notion, so well expressed by Plato, that the material world is only one of shadow and appearance, while the real world is one of pure ideas, of which material things are poor, faint images. This is the basis of the spiritualizing tendency which is still with us in some brands of Catholic theology and spirituality.

The Hebrew mind saw things as close to God because of their connection with the divine purpose for the universe – clearly identified by Jesus as the project of the Kingdom of God. Whether these things were material or immaterial was not the point. It is the use men and women make of their bodies and other material objects which determines how spiritual they are. 'Spiritual', in the biblical and theologically correct sense, is bound up with the Holy Spirit and not with Greek philosophical notions. Those objects and structures which are placed under the influence of the Spirit of God are spiritual, those which are removed from that influence and placed at the service of something else are sinful. It is always the human user who determines how spiritual things are. 'Spiritual' is not a philosophical quality of things but a theological category about relationships. In Paul's list of the 'works of the flesh' in Galatians 5 more than half of the items, such as 'envy, dissension and party-spirit', have nothing to do with matter. As in creation and in the incarnation, the Spirit of God produces corporeal life and makes human bodily life spiritual; Jesus Christ is the supreme example of this.

Over the centuries, some consensus emerges as to the necessary mediation of the humanity of Christ in contemplation. Unfortunately, this does not mean that in treating of the Mystery to be reached through mystagogy all theologians of spirituality speak in terms of the Mystery of Christ.

The historical origins of the Christian notion of mystery – and the origins of the biblical word *mystērion* – have not always been clear. The problem of the relation between the pagan mysteries and Christian beliefs arose during the nineteenth century due to philological and archaeological studies in the history of religion and to the decline in confidence as to the historical reliability of the Bible. Today it is generally accepted that Old Testament Jewish origins of the notion of mystery account for the New Testament, and especially Pauline, usage, more than any direct influence of the pagan mysteries.

The use of the word 'mystery' that became decisive for theology is the one adopted by St Paul. There is no longer any serious attempt to make out that he borrowed the word from the Greek mystery religions. It is clear to scholars that Paul is primarily dependent on Jewish sources for the notion.[23]

During the first half of the twentieth century there was much study and debate on the question, raised by specialists in the study of comparative religion, as to whether Christian sacramental rites were based on Greek mystery religion into which one entered through initiation. Odo Casel, the Benedictine monk of Maria Laach, attempted to agree as far as possible with the theory, seeing the sacraments as the *true* mysteries, as the perfect realization of a 'mystery model' of religion already existing, in outline, in paganism. Even though his theory is not much in vogue today, Odo Casel is to be thanked for reintroducing the ancient liturgical notion of mystery, with its experiential element, into a theology which had intellectualized the expression. He also drew attention to the central place of the Mystery of Christ's death and resurrection in Christian tradition.

In the second half of this century, the debate about the origins of *mystērion* has moved on to the attempt to see to what extent Christian liturgy grew out of Jewish religious rites and borrowed from them. The discovery of the Dead Sea Scrolls or Qumran texts in 1947 helped clarify the relationship between early Christianity and the Jewish religious traditions. Indeed, some see in the Khirbet Qumran Essenians a sect devoted to a mystery religion. Similarly, the Nag Hammadi library of ancient gnostic texts, dating from the fourth and fifth centuries AD, discovered in upper Egypt (in 1945), has helped scholars understand the shape and origins of primitive Christianity.

One of the fruits of the Second Vatican Council is the conviction that the Spirit of God is at work in the world from the beginning and prior to any evangelizing effort. This presence of God to all created things, especially the human, provides a backdrop to the specific work of redemption wrought by Jesus Christ. The relation between the two – creation and redemption – is not yet sufficiently developed theologically; certainly the liturgical tradition and the medieval mystics have much to offer in this domain. The consequences for missiology of the traditional but long forgotten truth of the action of the Spirit of God in the world since the beginning are enormous.

The style of mystagogy required to deal with experience of the creation dimension of the Mystery has been mentioned when dealing with the recovery of mystagogy and in connection with the names of Rahner, Schillebeeckx and Boff. Interest in and concern for ecology have a base in the theology of creation rather than in a directly christological theology. The unity of the two can be seen most clearly in the anticipated light of eschatology, all things being made new. In the last chapter of the Bible, the Genesis motifs of sun, moon and the tree of life with its fruits reappear alongside the transformed fruits of human labour in the holy city. Christ, seen in the hymn of Colossians as first-born of all creation, all things having been created in him and for him, reappears as Alpha and Omega. What began in an uncultivated garden ends in a perfect city, in which the best of creation mingles with the best of human handiwork, with Christ presiding over all.

The Mystery, as challenge to the faith of modern people and to the creativity and guidance of pastors, is identified as being inside the human situation of modern living, and not outside it. Modern living may be examined with the help of the human sciences but a reading in the light of faith is needed in order to appreciate the Mystery. There is not a mystery of the Church outside of and above the concrete, visible reality which can be studied by human wisdom.[24] It is the light of faith brought to bear on the visible reality which yields up the Mystery. Mystery is not mystification and is not to be invoked in order to remove things 'religious' from the scrutiny of ordinary mortals. Too often, attempts are made to justify arbitrary ways of acting and of structuring things ecclesial in terms of a level of mystery outside the concrete and visible and outside accountability to those not trained in theology.

Vatican II, in its Declaration on the Relation of the Church to Non-Christian Religions, included among the questions facing all humanity today: 'What is the ultimate mystery, beyond human explanation, which embraces our entire existence, from which we take our origin and towards which we tend?'[25]

Mystagogy means initiation into the *Mystery* and for a Christian the Mystery is the Mystery of Christ. In the Mystery of Christ there is a privileged moment, that of the Paschal Mystery of Christ's death and resurrection through which he became Lord of history and constructor of the Kingdom. The Mystery contains the saving events of Christ's career, all of which are celebrated in Christian liturgy. The eucharistic prayers of the current *Missale Romanum* (Roman Missal) make it clear that the future salvific event of Christ's Second Coming is also matter for celebration; in eucharistic prayers Three and Four, after Christ's words at the Last Supper, the anamnesis recalls to the participants what they are about, in a concise summary of the chief facets of the Mystery:

> Father, calling to mind the death your Son endured for our salvation, his glorious resurrection and ascension into heaven, and ready to greet him when he comes again, we offer you in thanksgiving this holy and living sacrifice . . .[26]

Scripturally and liturgically the paschal facet of the Christ event is privileged. It is the Paschal Mystery into which the Christian is baptized; it is that Mystery which is primarily celebrated in the Eucharist, primarily preached by the apostles, basically believed by every Christian.[27]

One of the key factors in the pastoral renewal which was made official at Vatican II was the restating of the central position of the one Mystery of the death, resurrection and ascension of Christ. It was a happy invention which hit on the expression 'Paschal Mystery' to express that centre. The expression 'Paschal Mystery' (*paschale mysterium*) is not, itself, traditional. It is a product of the liturgical movement of the first half of this century. The traditional expression, found in prayers of the Easter Vigil, is *paschale sacramentum*, an expression which dates back to Leo the Great. To go back from the Latin *sacramentum* to the Greek word *mystery* was quite legitimate and had, at that time, the advantage of avoiding the expression 'mystery', on its own, which was still not quite free from association with Greek pagan mysteries.

When the Council, in its first document, *Sacrosanctum Concilium*, the Constitution on the Liturgy, outlines the theology which is at the base of liturgical renewal, it uses the expression 'Paschal Mystery' to describe the centre of the Christ event in the work of our redemption:

> The wonderful works of God among the people of the Old Testament were but a prelude to the work of Christ Our Lord in redeeming mankind and giving perfect glory to God. He achieved his task principally by the paschal mystery of his blessed passion, resurrection from the dead, and glorious ascension, whereby 'dying, he destroyed our death, and rising, restored our life'.[28]

The Paschal Mystery is also highlighted as the focus towards which the Old Testament was a prelude. The paragraphs which follow show unequivocally the central place of the Paschal Mystery in Christian liturgy, and point out that the Eucharist, and all the sacraments of the Church, belong to the fruits of the Paschal Mystery in their work of sanctifying humanity and glorifying God. The liturgy is the pinnacle to which all the Church's action reaches out and the source from which it draws all its strength.

The repeated references to the Paschal Mystery in Vatican II amount to a positive statement as to the place of the death and resurrection of Jesus in Christian biblical, liturgical and patristic tradition. The Council Fathers made it clear that the Mystery makes present to believers the fullest reality of the work of salvation: and this in accord with doctrinal, liturgical and patristic tradition. Vatican II took up, reflected on and made official the best of the renewal thinking in the fields of Scripture, patristics and liturgy which had been pursued – sometimes without much encouragement from the magisterium – since the first half of the last century. All these disciplines coincide in giving the Paschal Mystery central place in Christian Revelation. The Council document on Revelation, *Dei Verbum*, outlines the task of theology as that of pondering, in the light of faith, the fullness of truth contained in the Mystery of Christ. Study of Scripture is the soul of theology:[29] hence theology should have as its centre what is central in the scriptural revelation.

As the liturgy is the original and privileged place of mystagogy, the Mystery into which the man or woman aspiring to become a Christian is to be initiated is primarily the Paschal Mystery. This is substantiated by the Vatican II document on the missions, *Ad Gentes*, which makes explicit mention of the stages in the process of conversion:

> From sin . . . into the mystery of God's love . . . Under the movement of divine grace the new convert sets out on a spiritual journey by means of which, while already sharing through faith in the mystery of the death and resurrection, he passes from the old man to the new man who has been made perfect in Christ.[30]

The mission document of the Council, quoted above, sees the conversion process as an initiation into, and a living of, the mystery of Christ's death and resurrection. *Ad Gentes* leaves no doubt but that it is into the Paschal Mystery of Christ that the candidates are initiated:

> Having been delivered from the powers of darkness through the sacraments of Christian initiation, and having died, been buried, and risen with Christ, they receive the Spirit of adoption of children and celebrate with the whole people of God the memorial of the Lord's death and resurrection.

It is desirable that the liturgy of Lent and Paschal time should be restored in such a way that it will serve to prepare the hearts of the catechumens for the celebration of the Paschal Mystery, at whose solemn ceremonies they are reborn to Christ in Baptism.[31]

In speaking of the Paschal Mystery, the Council says that it had a prelude in the *divina magnalia* of the Old Testament.[32] Chief among those 'wonderful works of God' was the Exodus, which biblical theology of recent generations has increasingly shown to be the centre and hinge of the entire Old Testament. The Exodus marked Israel's birth as a people and its choice as People of God. It was the foundation event of Israel's life as a nation and of its relation to God. The liturgy of Israel, especially the Passover, takes its origin from the Exodus event which it celebrates as a relived memory.

The Vatican II document on ecumenism makes the point[33] not only that, in ecumenical dialogue (and, by extension, in all presentation of Catholic belief), the integral Catholic doctrine must be expounded, but also that there exists a hierarchy of truths in the Catholic faith. Truths are important according to the degree they approach the foundation or basis of Christian faith. In judging of the authenticity of a mystical experience or a new form of spirituality, this teaching on the hierarchy of truths should be invoked. The closer a devotion or experience comes to the mystery of the Kingdom of God founded on Christ's death and resurrection, the more is its *prima facie* likelihood of being genuine or authentic. This criterion must be kept in mind while evaluating the mystagogy of any new ecclesial development. Mystagogy, which works out, in concentric circles, from the dynamic centre of all things Christian, is constructed entirely on the conviction not only that there exists 'a hierarchy of truths', but that, prior to truths, there is the one central reality of the Christ event: Jesus dead and risen and coming in his Kingdom. This central event of salvation history is prior to any account of it and to any theologizing about it. It is to lead men and women to an experience of that central Mystery that mystagogy aspires. If this experience of the Mystery is given its place, intellectual instruction can constitute an important backup. If experience of the Mystery is absent, intellectual instruction is no substitute.

The transformation of every facet and structure of human life belongs also to the domain of the Paschal Mystery, which not only symbolizes but effects the presence of God's Kingdom here on earth. In a section on the Paschal Mystery, the Latin American bishops at Puebla (1979) speak of Jesus Christ being constituted 'Lord of the world and of history', through his resurrection which is 'pledge of the ultimate transformation of the universe':[34]

The Kingdom of God, shining resplendently on the visage of the risen Jesus Christ, is already planted in the centre of human history. The justice of God has triumphed over the injustice of human beings. The old history began with Adam; with Jesus Christ, the new Adam, there begins a new history driven by an unfailing impetus. It will lead all human beings, made children of God through the efficacy of the Spirit, to ever more perfect dominion over the world, daily increasing fraternal communion, and the fullness of communion and participation that constitutes the very life of God. So we proclaim the Good News of the person of Jesus Christ to the people of Latin America, who are called to be new human beings in the newness of baptism and life according to the Gospel. This should sustain their efforts and nurture their hope.[35]

While insisting on the transcendent aspects of the Kingdom, theology now takes account of the necessary contribution of men and women to its construction. In *Redemptoris Missio*, his encyclical on the missions (1990), Pope John Paul II has this to say:

The Kingdom is the concern of everyone: individuals, society, and the world. Working for the Kingdom means acknowledging and promoting God's activity, which is present in human history and transforms it. Building the Kingdom means working for liberation from evil in all its forms. In a word, the Kingdom of God is the manifestation and the realization of God's plan of salvation in all its fullness. (no. 15)

Catholic liturgy has long linked the perspective of the Kingdom (and Christ's kingship) with the Paschal Mystery; one way it has done this is by celebrating, at the opening of Holy Week, Christ's entrance into Jerusalem. The Palm Sunday liturgy combines commemoration of the non-violent, triumphal entry of the Messiah-King into the city of the warrior king David with present celebration of Christ's entry into our cities and the promise of our common entry into the heavenly Jerusalem with him when he comes again. The celebration – as in all true liturgy – has a tri-directional reference: to an historical past event in salvation history; to a present, lived sacramentally; and to a future 'end time', to be striven for in hope. Palm Sunday commemorates the past, historical event, while it re-actualizes it in the present by a renewal of commitment to Christ as Lord of history today, and anticipates, in hope, his taking definitive possession of his Kingdom of the Holy City of the New Jerusalem. Something of the same joining of Kingdom and Paschal motifs occurs in every eucharistic prayer of the Roman Mass. When we meet to celebrate the Eucharist we repeat the cry of the crowd on the occasion of Jesus' entry into Jerusalem, 'Hosanna! Blessed is he who comes in the name of the Lord! Blessed is the kingdom of our father David that is coming! Hosanna in the highest!' (Mark 11:9–10).

The revelation of the New Jerusalem in the final chapters of the Apocalypse is not an excuse to escape work here and now to transform our world into some adumbration of the Kingdom: it is a greater incentive to undertake that effort. The fact that we are co-heirs with Christ to an eternal Kingdom does not exempt us from struggling to improve this world; rather it spurs us on to that struggle. It is in the Mystery of Christ, made Lord of history through his resurrection, that the apparent contradiction between work for the progress of humanity and work for the coming of God's Kingdom is resolved.[36] The Church is badly served by the theological myopia of those who ignore the early history of the Church, and who cannot see any horizon of tradition extending back beyond Trent. Others limit their vision in a way that is equally damaging: they work for the change of political and economic structures, without situating that effort within the full scope of salvation history, to which its future and final phase is integral.

Now that the central position of the Mystery of Christ has been recovered, it is time to recover also that mystagogy which makes initiation into experience of that central Mystery the main work of religious formation. Such formation must be attentive to developments in the theology of creation and must stay attuned to the concerns of today's people, especially the young, who are tomorrow's people.

Many young people in countries of ancient Catholic culture have become disillusioned with a Church which tries to hold on to the past in formality, ritual and a dated individualistic morality. When they meet a Church that is youthful and close to the concerns of the people, especially the poor, they begin to see some relevance for a religion which they had felt was an obstacle to living the values preached and witnessed by Jesus Christ. Because of the stance of too many clerics, the name of Jesus Christ, identified with an antiquated looking institution, had become an obstacle to experiencing God. When Catholicism was experienced as joyful service of the poor – Good News of social justice, human rights or simple human sympathy – they came to know another Jesus to whom they could relate. Experience of the Gospel in action, with a minimum of discourse, revealed to them something of the coming Kingdom.

NOTES

1   Cf. G. Bornkamm, '*Mystērion*' in Kittel, 1- vol. edn, pp. 615–19.
2   H. Cazelles, 'Le mystère de la présence de Dieu dans l'Ancien Testament' in A. M. Triacca and A. Pistoia (eds), *Mystagogie: Pensée liturgique d'aujourd'hui et liturgie ancienne* (Rome: Edizioni Liturgiche, 1993), p. 69.
3   Ibid., pp. 69–72.

4   *SC* 106. There are two distinct 'mystagogic' explanations of the Sabbath in the Old Testament: one, the priestly one, insists on the Sabbath rest in imitation of Yahweh's rest at the end of the work of creation (Exod 20:8–11); the other links the Sabbath rest to freedom from slavery in Egypt (Deut 5:12–15), where the Israelites had to work from dawn to dusk every day until they dropped. The Sabbath rest is a celebration of freedom from slavery to work – seen as the total meaning of the worker's existence. The first of these explanations is linked to the order of creation, the second to the order of redemption, foreshadowing the unity between Paschal Mystery and Kingdom.

5   *SC* 102–103.

6   K. McDonnell and G. T. Montague, *Christian Initiation and Baptism in the Holy Spirit* (Collegeville: Liturgical Press, 1991). This aspect of the Christian Mystery traditionally provided the model for the baptism of Christians and explained the gift (and experience) of the Spirit, which (for adults) was long seen as integral to that initiation.

7   D. Bosch, *Transforming Mission* (Maryknoll, NY: Orbis, 1991), p. 78.

8   Colossians 1:13–14, 18.

9   Cf. P. J. Kobelski, 'The Letter to the Ephesians', *The New Jerome Biblical Commentary* (Englewood Cliffs, NJ: Prentice Hall/London: Geoffrey Chapman, 1990), p. 884.

10 Ephesians 3:4–6.

11 E. Mazza, *Mystagogy* (New York: Pueblo, 1989), pp. 22–3.

12 K. McDonnell and G. T. Montague, *Christian Initiation*, p. 187. The title of McDonnell's relevant chapter (14) is 'Cyril of Jerusalem: from outside the mystery to inside'.

13 G. Friedrich, '*Kēryssō, Kērygma*' in Kittel, 1-vol. edn, pp. 434–5.

14 Cf. K. Rahner, 'The concept of mystery in Catholic theology' in *Theological Investigations* 4 (London: Darton, Longman & Todd, 1966), pp. 37–43.

15 Du Cange, *Glossarium Mediae et Infimae Latinitatis* (Paris, 1938), vol. 5, has no entry for *mystagogia*; and even the texts cited under *mysterium* frequently reveal confusion between this term and *ministerium*.

16 For liturgical specialists, such as Joseph Jungmann, the feast of the Trinity is an 'idea feast', that is, it results from theological speculation, sparked off by the Arian controversy, and is not one of the historical events in the saving work of Christ: J. A. Jungmann, *Liturgisches Erbe und Pastorale Gegenwart*: Eng. trans. *Pastoral Liturgy* (London: Challoner Publications, 1962), pp. 396–7. An older tradition, which included the Baptism of Jesus in the Creed, saw that event as a manifestation of the Trinity: cf. K. McDonnell and G. T. Montague, *Christian Initiation*, p. 246. Montague even thinks it likely that Jesus' command to baptize in the name of the Trinity, in Matthew 28:19, is due to seeing 'Christian baptism as a participation in Jesus' own experience in the Jordan' (p. 19).

17 K. Young, *The Drama of the Medieval Church* (Oxford: Oxford University Press, 1933), vol. 2, pp. 421f.

18 E. C. Dunn, 'Drama, medieval' in *New Catholic Encyclopedia* 4, pp. 1039–48.

19 K. Rahner, 'The concept of mystery in Catholic theology' in *Theological Investigations* 4, pp. 36–73. Rahner agrees with calling the pre-Vatican II Scholastic theology of mystery 'a complicated dogmatic system too knowledgeable by far, too clever, rationalistic and positivist, too ready to lay down the law . . .': p. 37.

20 K. Rahner, ibid., p. 65.
21 K. Rahner, 'Remarks on the dogmatic treatise "De Trinitate"' in *Theological Investigations* 4, p. 87.
22 K. Rahner, ibid., p. 98. Similar ideas are to be found in 'The concept of mystery in Catholic theology' in *Theological Investigations* 4, pp. 69–71. While Rahner does not always complete his expositions on God with an explicitly christological treatment, he is aware of the need for this, cf. 'Christian living formerly and today' in *Theological Investigations* 7 (London: Darton, Longman & Todd, 1971), p. 16, note 12.
23 Cf. R. E. Brown, *The Semitic Background of the Term Mystery in the New Testament* (Philadelphia: Fortress, 1968).
24 E. Schillebeeckx, *Church: The Human Story of God* (London: SCM, 1990), p. 213.
25 *Nostra Aetate* 1: 'Quid demum illud ultimum et ineffabile mysterium quod nostram existentiam amplectitur, ex quo ortum sumus et quo tendimus?'
26 *Missale Romanum*, Eucharistic Prayer III.
27 In his biography, *Paul VI, First Modern Pope* (London: HarperCollins, 1993), Peter Hebblethwaite recalls (p. 531) that the name of the *motu proprio* introducing the new Roman Missal, fruit of Vatican II liturgical renewal, has for its title *Mysterii Paschali*, and adds the comment that this title 'was chosen to show that the whole purpose of liturgical reform was to bring out the absolute centrality of the whole Paschal mystery, cross and resurrection, in Christian life'.
28 *SC* 5.
29 *DV* 24.
30 *AG* 13.
31 *AG* 14.
32 *SC* 5.
33 Vatican II, *Unitatis Redintegratio* 11.
34 Puebla 195.
35 Puebla 197.
36 Cf. Vatican II, *GS* 39, 45, 72.

8

INITIATION AND INCULTURATION

MYSTAGOGY AND INITIATION

According to Justin Martyr we are born 'children of necessity and ignorance', and by baptism we become 'children of knowledge and election'. It is this passing from a natural state to one of choice that calls for initiation and conversion. The transition to the Christian Mystery takes on a relatively stable form and the conversion which it involves is given shape by the Church. Judaism had also its initiation rites and it seems likely that the Jewish structures for the preparation of proselytes provided the chief model for early Christian efforts. If the language used for Christian initiation, from the fourth century onwards, was that of the mystagogy of the traditional mystery religions, the theology and process owed more to Judaism.

Christians of early centuries rejected the idea that their initiation derived from initiation into pagan mysteries. Pagan mysteries were seen as diabolic imitations in advance of, or parallel to, Christian sacred rites. And during their last, dying years, the mysteries borrowed from Christian rites as much and perhaps more than did the Christians borrow from them, so that mutual suspicion was the order of the day. Once the Christian catechumenate became organized and catechumens were separated from the faithful, the borrowed vocabulary of initiation began to be regularly used.

Of the Fathers who deal with the topic of mystagogy, John Chrysostom speaks most of initiation. The expression for initiation into the mystery (mystagogy) was used by Chrysostom for the sacramental initiation, or occasionally for the baptismal immersion itself. For Chrysostom mystagogy refers to the rite of initiation itself (most usually the sacramental celebration of initiation), and never to any word about the rites spoken before or after their celebration. With Cyril of Jerusalem, in contrast, the vocabulary of initiation is used, not of the rites themselves, but of the series of homilies which follows on the rites of initiation. So that, since the Fathers differ in their use of the expression 'mystagogy', we are free to follow Chrysostom and apply the expression to the initiation as more than 'pre-' or 'post-' sacramental catechesis.[1]

It is not certain that the arrangement arrived at by the *Ordo* for the Christian Initiation of Adults (RCIA) is the best one: placing mystagogy at the end of the initiation, and only speaking of it there, makes it look as though mystagogy is an afterthought of a primarily intellectual nature, thus prolonging the intellectualization of 'religious education', so long deplored. Mystagogy was originally understood of the entire process of conducting the candidate through the initiation so as to have him or her arrive at the deepest experience of the (Greek or Roman) mystery. There could be a much richer understanding of mystagogy if it were considered to be one *level* – that of experience – rather than a last *period* in a whole which is nowadays too easily dominated by the type of learning proper to the stage of catechesis.

We come here to the relationship of Christian sacraments and experience to non-Christian rites or experience, and more fundamentally to the scope of the incarnation. It is agreed today that the Christian sacraments are not, historically, borrowings from the mystery rites and that, theologically, they are quite different in purpose. This does not necessarily mean that there is no anthropological human base that would allow the divine to touch the deepest reaches of the human person through the symbolism of the sacrament. With Vatican II the dualisms derived from pagan Greek philosophy were exorcized. Some have let them in the back door again. *Gaudium et Spes* admits only one history of the world – and that belongs to God – leaving behind the notion of a sacred history running parallel to secular history.[2]

What anthropologists (many of them missionaries) have taught us about 'primitive' peoples and their religions alters the way we look on other religions. Few or none of these peoples considered 'pagan' lack all knowledge of the Creator and source of life. What we know of their beliefs, myths and rites can teach us much about our own religious outlook, the symbols we employ and our use of ritual. What we lack is a theological method adequate to using anthropology (and the other 'sciences of the human'). It is only in the Latin American Theology of Liberation that the 'see, judge, act' approach of *Gaudium et Spes*, which was praised in *Sollicitudo Rei Socialis* in 1987 as theologically sound for use in moral questions, has been systematically employed as a way of thinking theologically about matters studied by the social sciences. This theological approach starts from the situation under consideration, read in the light of the conclusions of a social science and then illuminated by the light of faith in order to decide on action. In the case of the initiation process in peoples of pre-modern culture, the social science would be anthropology. For lack of some such method, studies that treat theologically of cultural differences all too often hijack anthropological terms without respecting the character of the science from which they appropriated them. Some use of analogy is made at times, but again this tends to be a reductive use of the science in question.[3]

Some liturgists see the sacraments as so much more important than any 'merely' human and psychological accompaniment, that, for them, such 'preparation' may equally well come after as before the sacramental celebration. This would seem to be an exalting of the sacraments above the human order of things and a playing down of the human practice of initiation. Reacting against any comparison with non-Christian initiations, these liturgists fail to appreciate the place of the social and the human in the sacramental system. Part and parcel of this view is the hope that any revision of the *Ordo initiationis christianae adultorum* will adopt the idea that the sacramental celebration itself (with its purely 'spiritual' experience, independent of anything human) is the initiation and that anything else is secondary.[4] It seems to be this emphasis that allows the 'catechumenate' to be shifted around at will.

Instead of considering mystagogy as one moment of the initiation, it could be considered as a *level* of the entire initiation process. Evangelization and *kerygma* do not imply a first intellectual contact with Christ: they can and should have their mystagogical dimension of an introduction to the experience of the Christian Mystery in the person of Christ. The insistence on complete doctrinal teaching at one moment, and mystical illumination at another, may not be the most effective way of underlining the importance of experience of the Mystery. The mystery – *sacramentum* – is itself an important element in the initiation; mystagogy applies to it too. The whole initiation process should be thought of as mystagogic, and not only the last stage in it, while special attention to this dimension at one chronological moment makes good pastoral sense.

Faith does not consist in knowledge alone, but involves entering with heart and body, imagination and feeling, into a network where the corporeal, symbolic and social dimensions are essential. As Vatican II says, 'By the gift of the Holy Spirit, man comes, through faith, to contemplate and savour the mystery of God's design'.[5] A life of faith is a life which is dynamic and full of energy. It was Scholastic theology which made faith a purely intellectual act of assent – little less than absurd, as Joseph Comblin says.[6] So, also, initiation may be seen to have several necessary elements or dimensions: catechetic, community, ritual and sacramental.

The term 'initiation' does not always indicate a particular moment, nor even a ceremony, at which a person passes from being a catechumen to being one of the 'faithful'. Initiation is frequently given a broader meaning which takes in the whole process of growth, lasting for some time (perhaps several years) and including all the factors involved in the journey to a personal and adult identity as member of the community. To speak of initiation in this sense is to describe how an individual, in the proper setting, with the necessary support, achieves a Christian identity which becomes part of him or her as a gift of the Lord.[7]

It is easy to overlook the fact that other religions, some of them of venerable antiquity and having sacred texts, also had, and still have, 'rites and symbols of initiation'.[8] Due to the predominant influence exercised by the Greco-Roman culture on Christian thinking, we have been considering initiation in the Christian and classical pre-Christian contexts. Whatever the significance of that influence in the past, now that we are consciously entering a pluralistic and multicultural age, we need to learn from the traditional religions and cultures which still survive the assaults of First World patterns.

Mircea Eliade points out – as fruit of his outstanding studies in the history of religions – that 'initiation is coexistent with any re-evaluation of spiritual life'. He uses this argument to suggest that Christianity could well have 'invented' initiatory rites quite independently of the mystery religions of Greece and Rome. This denial of any need for imitation of pre-existing rites is only possible because any new evaluation of spiritual life is accompanied by initiation. According to Eliade, 'All pre-modern societies . . . accord primary importance to the ideology and techniques of initiation'. He defines initiation as:

> A body of rites and oral teachings whose purpose is to produce a decisive alteration in the religious and social status of the person to be initiated.

He goes on to say that:

> Every primitive society possesses a consistent body of mythical traditions, a 'conception of the world'; and it is this conception that is gradually revealed to the novice in the course of his initiation. The majority of initiatory ordeals more or less clearly imply a ritual death followed by resurrection or new birth . . .

> He returns to life a new man, assuming another mode of being. Initiatory death signifies the end at once of childhood, ignorance, and of the profane condition.

Initiation is of such importance for a knowledge of pre-modern man. It reveals the almost awesome seriousness with which the man of archaic societies assumed the responsibility of receiving and transmitting spiritual values.

Eliade goes on to show how initiation represents one of the most significant phenomena in the history of humanity, involving, as it does, not only the religious life of the person, but the entire life of that man or woman:

It is through initiation that, in primitive and archaic societies, man becomes what he is and what he should be – a being open to the life of the spirit, hence one who participates in the culture into which he was born . . . Through initiation, the candidate passes beyond the natural mode – the mode of the child – and gains access to the cultural mode; that is, he is introduced to spiritual values. From a certain point of view it could almost be said that, for the primitive world, it is through initiation that men attain the status of human beings . . .

Initiation . . . is a fundamental existential experience because through it a man becomes able to assume his mode of being in its entirety.[9]

These passages quoted from Eliade remind us to be careful in our use of expressions like 'pagan' for those who are not Christian, as though those peoples had no valid knowledge of God or of things spiritual. Eliade's studies also remind us that the Christian Church has initiated only a small portion of the human race, and that portion does not always include those peoples whose cultures were marked by the highest spiritual values. In African cultures the notion of the human person includes the element of continual growth or development, a process in which initiation holds a prominent place. Completion of the personality is achieved only gradually and through relationships. Among these relationships, the rites of initiation play an irreplaceable role. Initiation is built into the development of the self and is not something extra which may or may not be added on.

In the passage from Eliade, quoted above, he speaks of initiation among peoples of pre-modern cultures. Now, as we enter an age following on the modern, and no longer enchanted by the absolute power of reason, it is becoming clear that the young of the cultures of our industrialized world are in need of initiation into adulthood. At present there is a growing awareness of the need for initiation into adult life for young people in the countries of consumer culture, just as much as for those in traditional cultures. Passage from the home-based trade or craft to factory or huge office-block has made it more difficult for young people to experience the adult world in which their parents live and work. As well as making relations with father and mother more difficult, this absence of the adult makes the process of growing up – passing from the natural to the cultural mode of existence – more difficult too. For the achieving of adult male identity – made more difficult by necessary recent insistence on female values in some countries – Robert Bly has written *Iron John*, a poetic and ancient-myth based book on this problem of the need for 'initiation into male spirit':

> The ancient societies believed that a boy becomes a man only through ritual and effort – only through the 'active intervention of the older men'.[10]

Bly suggests paths towards achieving such initiation into adulthood. Regrettably, the emphasis is on the individual rather than on the community. Indirectly the community enters, as when Bly points out that gangs of young people are a spurious imitation of initiation and not an adequate substitute for contact with adults in the process of growing up. Drug-taking can be seen as an attempt to precipitate experience and gain ecstasy which have not come about through maturing. The young person has to learn to break the links of childhood dependency on his or her parents without doing damage to self in the process.[11]

The theological principle that grace builds on nature still holds. No one can be or become an adult and mature Christian if that person has never become a mature adult human being. It is true that both processes may advance together. But it should be clear that no process of learning doctrine can alone make for Christian maturity if human maturity has not been achieved[12] or if the basic experience of contact with adult Christians is lacking. The roles of witness, of Godparents, of the adult community, are irreplaceable.

MYSTAGOGY AND INCULTURATION

Inculturation is a topical theme, vital to any discussion of Christian mission. But its relevance extends also to the Church in lands of ancient Christianity. The excessive role of Greco-Roman culture in Catholic theology calls for an inculturation of theology into the contemporary world that is distancing itself more and more from classical ways of thinking and acting. At the time of Vatican II, cultural change was the reason for the irrelevance of the Church in the eyes of contemporary men and women. Pope John felt this and convoked the Council to meet the challenge, which was not so much doctrinal error as pastoral inadequacy. Although the term, already coined, had not come into common use, 'inculturation' was what the Second Vatican Council was all about.[13] Technological change had helped produce cultural patterns in the industrialized world that prevailing pastoral structures were unable to meet. In the lands recently freed from the colonial yoke, recognition of the rich diversity of their autonomous cultures was dawning. This contributed towards altering the whole approach to mission. Inculturation loomed as a priority challenge. This challenge is central to the question of initiation.

Mystagogy now means introducing people to the depths of the Mystery of Christ, but it originally meant leading candidates into an experience of the divine in the mystery religions of Greece and Rome. It was through a daring and singularly successful operation of inculturation that the Church adopted the language of mystagogy, while applying it to its own specific structures of initiation. The divinity, the Mystery into which the candidates were introduced, and the steps of the initiation were changed.

In apostolic times and throughout the patristic age, the Church adapted its initiation rites and procedures to persons, times and places. A dialectic involving the Mystery and the neophytes was constantly being worked out. The period of the classical catechumenate and liturgy of initiation (fourth to sixth centuries) leaves us an example of the insertion of Christianity in the culture of the Greco/Roman Empire. So successful was this inculturation into the Greco-Roman world that we tend to canonize that cultural complex, as though it had the same sort of privileged position as has the biblical culture of ancient Israel. Indeed, even the culture of Israel, though privileged for an understanding of the Bible, is not to be imposed on other peoples. Israel may have been called to bring other peoples into its cultural fold: no part of the Christian Church is called to do this. On the contrary, Christians have received the Spirit of Jesus so as to be able to incarnate his Kingdom in each cultural setting and in each age.

When pastoral conditions changed and the initiation of adults became a rarity, mystagogy was forgotten for more than a millennium. New cultural circumstances have recently contributed to produce men and women for whom old ways of assimilating the Christian faith are obsolete, and for whom classical spiritual language is irrelevant. Some theologians have come up with suggestions for a new style of mystagogy, relevant to the cultural milieu of industrialized, middle-class, urban men and women. It is that style which we have called mystagogy for the Christian in the world of today. In other parts of the world, a different style of mystagogy will be called for.

Some constants and some variables can usefully be identified in this process: *Gaudium et Spes* devoted a whole chapter to the question of culture. It said:

> It is one of the properties of the human person that he can achieve true and full humanity only by means of culture . . . The word

'culture' in the general sense refers to all those things which go to the refining and developing of man's diverse mental and physical endowments.[14]

The Vatican International Theological Commission (CTI) document on *Faith and Inculturation* (1989) says that: 'The incarnation of the Son of God was a cultural incarnation', and quotes *Ad Gentes*: 'Christ, in virtue of his incarnation, bound himself to the definite social and cultural conditions of those human beings among whom he dwelt'.[15] The CTI goes on to say that:

> Jesus is so bound up with the life of Israel that the people and the religious tradition in which he shares acquire in virtue of this liaison a unique place in the history of salvation; this chosen people and the religious tradition which they have left have a permanent significance for humanity . . . the history of the covenant concluded with Abraham and through Moses with the people of Israel, as also the books which recount and clarify this history, all together hold for the faithful of Jesus the role of an indispensable and irreplaceable pedagogy.[16]

'The word "inculturation" . . . can be seen as the contraction of the expression "insertion in a culture".'[17] Vatican II, while not using the word 'inculturation', described the missionary process in terms which would now call for the use of the expression:

> If the Church is to be in a position to offer all men the mystery of salvation and the life brought by God, then it must implant itself among all these groups in the same way that Christ by his incarnation committed himself to the particular social and cultural circumstances of the men among whom he lived.[18]

Mystagogy presupposes inculturation: the people to be initiated must have contact with Christ and his Mystery in cultural terms which they can understand and appreciate. Their experience must be a real one that touches their lives. Mystagogy is the initiating, done by the Spirit, in the Church, through the instrumentality of rites and with the help of mystagogues. This means that the language of the Bible, the experience of Christian witness and the help of the mystagogue must be accessible to that people. This rendering accessible of the Christian message and of Christ living in his Church, for each era and in each cultural area, is the work of inculturation.

Ad Gentes speaks of inculturation in the context of offering the 'mystery' of salvation. This suggests a parallel between inculturation of the Mystery of Christ in a hitherto unchristianized culture, and the mystagogic task of helping the individual convert penetrate the depths of the same Mystery.

Modern hermeneutics teaches that the Word of God must constantly be read and reread if we are to discover its message for our personal and social context. When an individual or a whole people is to be helped to come into saving contact with the living Mystery, attention must be given not only to the hermeneutical demands of the biblical texts and ecclesial tradition, but also to the cultural demands of the neophytes.

At the earliest Christian turning-point, difference in culture was central. The decision, at Jerusalem, presented in Acts 15, and the tensions which preceded this moment, hinged on the cultural differences between Christians come from Judaism and converts from among the Gentiles. The period of Judeo-Christianity prior to the 'Council of Jerusalem' has been counted by Karl Rahner as the first of only three periods which he considers to cover theologically the entire history of the Church to date.[19] In Rahner's schema the three periods are determined by cultural considerations:

1. The short period of Judeo-Christianity;

2. The period of the Church in a particular cultural group, that of Hellenism and European culture and civilization;

3. The period (beginning with Vatican II) in which the Church's living space is from the very outset the whole world.[20]

Looking back on the achievements of the Second Vatican Council, Rahner identified the emergence of the World Church as the first new theologically discerned period in Christian history since Constantine.

Variants on the theme have been put forward. The presentation of the Christian message to the Greek world necessarily differed from its presentation to the Jewish world; this has been considered as the 'basic inculturation', joining in the one Church Christians from Judaism with those converted from paganism. The next historical stages in inculturation would then be:

*   the inculturation of a minority Christianity in a society which was for the greater part pagan;

*   from the fourth century, the fusion of the cultural heritage of antiquity, with the now majority Christianity;

*   the meeting of Christianity with new cultures.[21]

The present age must be counted among the new cultural epochs in which the Church has to continue its work of initiation into the Mystery of Christ. Change and cultural pluriformity were among the factors which prompted the convocation of the Second Vatican Council: a Church better adapted to facing those contemporary challenges was to result from the Council.[22] *Gaudium et Spes* takes up this theme of culture, and recalls periods during which the

Christian message was expressed in the concepts and language of different peoples.[23]

Speaking of contemporary culture, the International Theological Commission (CTI) says:

> The inculturation of the Gospel in modern societies will demand a methodical effort of concerted research and action . . . A receptive attitude is required among those who wish to understand and evangelize the world of our time . . . How should one make this (modern) man understand the radical nature of the message of Christ: unconditional love, evangelical poverty . . .? How should one arouse faith and hope in the event of the resurrection accomplished by Jesus Christ? . . . We must develop the capacity to analyse cultures and to gauge their moral and spiritual indicators.[24]

Vatican II suggested the method of handling this pastoral task. The *Gaudium et Spes* approach, now become standard for pastoral planning, is applicable to inculturation too. The starting-point is the concrete situation of the local people; this situation is examined with the help of the human sciences and then reflected on in the light of faith. In the case of a culture, the human science used in the analysis is anthropology. The local culture, known through contact with the people and systematized with the help of anthropology, is examined in the light of the Mystery of Christ to gauge its moral and spiritual indicators. These are the 'see' and 'judge' stages of the pastoral approach to theology. There is nothing to prevent members of a local religion being involved in this as part of inter-faith dialogue; though the task of inculturation belongs primarily to the Christian community. Decisions as to concrete action follow ('act'). If spiritual or theological *rapprochement* proves possible, steps to help members of the other faith experience something of the Christian Mystery might be worked out. The present suggestion concerns the place at which inculturation might employ some technical knowledge of anthropology. The same method is used when employing other social sciences like economics, history or sociology in a pastoral reflection aimed at more effective action.

The approach outlined above speaks of pastoral work with people of other faiths; it is equally valid for work with a new generation in the industrialized world. Their culture is so different from that of their parents that without inculturation they can scarcely meet the Gospel. Pastoral planning today needs anthropological knowledge of the cultural world of young men and women of this generation. The real situation of the dispossessed cannot be plumbed without the help of economics and sociology; the feminist struggle requires knowledge of history, sociology and psychology. Anthropology is needed to bridge the culture gap. The 'capacity to analyse cultures', mentioned in the above quotation from the CTI document on inculturation, cannot be developed without the help of anthropology.

The potential for touching contemporary hearts will be enhanced or diminished by the depth or superficiality of the theology we invoke in our inculturation. Reliance on the central Mystery of Christ brings the power of the Spirit to bear on a new cultural situation. An attempt to mention every facet of theological truth may only confuse and dishearten; inculturation as evangelization concerns the central mystery of our faith and not the trimmings. Once inter-cultural contact is established in relation to an experience of what is central, anything else that is needed can be supplied later; if the centre has not been secured in a lived experience, the rest will continue to be irrelevant.

As times changed, insistence on detail led to irrelevance and new generations of candidates to faith were not catered for. To start from the situation of the hearer is an attempt to remedy the imbalance. There is a delicate balance between stress on tradition, which leads to fundamentalism, and surrender to the 'situation', as having exclusive importance, which produces over-insistence on subjective elements.[25] In the present culture of experience, yesterday's theology comes across as fundamentalism, and for practical purposes of contemporary religious formation, it is. Theology exists for pastoral purposes and when it ceases to be pastorally relevant it belongs in a museum.

The CTI document emphasizes that 'The Holy Spirit does not establish a superculture'.[26] It is well to have this clear declaration from Cardinal Ratzinger's group of theologians. Sometimes Churches far from the centre have the impression that the Greco-Roman culture, which helped incarnate the Gospel for so many centuries, is unduly privileged. They feel that their cultures are taken less seriously.[27] At the three yearly Assembly of the Symposium of Episcopal Conferences of Africa and Madagascar (SECAM), held in Lagos, Nigeria, in 1987, a working paper pointed out that Rome holds a primacy of charity in the Church, but not a primacy of culture.

To respect this new, culturally conditioned situation of so many peoples is a challenge facing the Church for the third millennium. In the light of the growing realization that Christian failure in Asia is due to unwillingness to take inculturation seriously, the challenge becomes daunting indeed. The continent which produced all the world's great religions still houses 85 per cent of the world's non-Christians and has a population less than 2 per cent Christian. It is the area where mysticism is at home and from which the mystery cults, which gave rise to mystagogy, almost certainly had their origins. It is not through Western theology that Asia will come to know Jesus Christ but through a dialogue in which the quality of initiation into the Christian Mystery has a central role to play.

Religious formators in the industrialized world can profit from the intuitions of inculturation for their mystagogic task of leading young men and women to an experience of the Mystery of Christ. One intuition is that the mystagogue is the first person who must undergo a conversion. When the culture gap between one generation and another is as wide as it is today, anyone who wishes to lead the younger generation must first enter their culture, must be open to contemporary mentalities and values. The day of imparting universal and timeless truths is done. Unless the cultural language (not just of words, but of symbols and myths) is first learned, access to the thought world of those to be influenced is not possible. For too long those who prided themselves on 'knowing' spoke down to those considered ignorant.[28] Today it is easier to appreciate that everyone 'knows' something, especially if experience is accepted as the more important part of 'knowledge'. Before presuming to lead anyone anywhere, it is imperative to discover who they are and where. This demands change in the pedagogue, first of all.

NOTES

1 P.-M. Gy, 'La notion chrétienne d'initiation', *LMD* 132 (1977), pp. 33–54; P. De Roten, 'Le vocabulaire mystagogique de Saint Jean Chrysostome' in A. M. Triacca and A. Pistoia (eds), *Mystagogie: Pensée liturgique d'aujourd'hui et liturgie ancienne* (Rome: Edizioni Liturgiche, 1993), pp. 115–35.

2 *GS* 45: 'The Lord is the goal of human history, the focal point of the desires of history and civilization, the centre of mankind . . .'; cf. M.-D. Chenu, 'Pour une anthropologie sacramentelle', *LMD* 119 (1974), p. 98.

3 Cf. M.-D. Chenu, art. cit., pp. 87–8. The document of the International Theological Commission (CTI), *Faith and Inculturation* II, 12 (*AG* 10), English version: *Origins* vol. 18, no. 47 (4 May 1989), does not make explicit its method in employing anthropological terms.

4 A. M. Triacca, 'Terminologie initiatique ou mystagogique selon le Rituel de l'Initiation Chrétienne des Adultes' in A. M. Triacca and A. Pistoia (eds), *Mystagogie*, pp. 329–50; on p. 348 Triacca says '. . . Il sera bon de retenir comme définitivement acquis que ce qu'on appelle *sacrements de l'initiation chrétienne* constitue effectivement l'initiation elle-même'.

5 *GS* 15.

6 J. Comblin, *The Holy Spirit and Liberation* (London: Burns & Oates/Maryknoll, NY: Orbis, 1989), chapter 2.

7 L. Maldonado and D. Power, Editorial, *Concilium* 142 (1979).

8 The phrase is the title of a work by M. Eliade, *Rites and Symbols of Initiation: The Mysteries of Birth and Rebirth* (New York: Harper, 1958).

9 Ibid., p. 3.

10 R. Bly, *Iron John: A Book About Men* (New York: Random House, 1992), p. 14. Cf. also, from a psychologist's point of view, G. Corneau, *Absent Fathers, Lost Sons*, trans. from French (Boston and London: Shambhala, 1991).

11 Current criticism of initiatory rites into some student, military, police or other corporations shows little or no appreciation of this anthropological need and might be relativized in the light of the research done by Bly and others.

12   Insistence on sacramental celebration without accompanying growth as a human being can lead to the caricatures of holiness sometimes encountered, where faith is thought to make up for a man or woman being less than human.

13   The first published use of the term 'inculturation' is usually given as R. P. Segura OP, 'L'initiation valeur permanente de l'inculturation', *Museon Lessianum*, Section missiologique 40 (1959), pp. 219–35.

14   *GS* 53: 'omnia quibus homo multifarias dotes animi corporisque perpolit atque explicat'. Since *Gaudium et Spes* was drafted in French, it may be useful to give the phrase in that language: 'tout ce par quoi l'homme affine et développe les multiples capacités de son esprit et de son corps . . .'.

15   CTI, *Faith and Inculturation*, II, 12, English version, p. 804.

16   Ibid., II, 15, 17.

17   A. Roest Crollius, 'What is so new about inculturation?' in A. Roest Crollius (ed.), *What Is So New About Inculturation?* (Rome: PUG, 1984), p. 4.

18   *AG* 10.

19   K. Rahner, 'Basic theological interpretation of the Second Vatican Council' in *Theological Investigations* 20 (London: Darton, Longman & Todd, 1981), pp. 82f.

20   Ibid., p. 83.

21   Cf. P. Y.-M. Gy, 'The inculturation of the Christian liturgy in the West', one of the papers of the *Societas Liturgica* Congress held in York, Great Britain (August 1989) on 'The Inculturation of the Liturgy'.

22   Significant phrases from Pope John's opening address to Vatican II, 11 October 1962, show his pastoral concern at the needs of changing times: *Sacrosanctum Oecumenicum Concilium Vaticanum II, Constitutiones Decreta Declarationes* (Rome: Vatican, 1965), 'Summi Pontificis Ioannis XXIII Allocutio in Solemni SS: Concilii Inauguratione:

  . . . hominum societas novum rerum ordinem ingredi videtur . . . (859) has novas inductas rerum condiciones . . . (860) . . . at simul necesse habet, ut praesentia quoque aspiciat tempora, quae novas induxerunt rerum condiciones, novasque vitae formas, atque nova catholico apostolatui patefecerunt itinera . . . (862) . . . oportet ut haec doctrina certa et immutabilis . . . ea ratione pervestigetur et exponatur, quam tempora postulant nostra . . . (865): Divine Providence is leading us to a new order of human relations . . . these new conditions of modern life . . . she must ever look to the present, to the new conditions and new forms of life introduced into the modern world which have opened new avenues to the Catholic apostolate . . . the whole world expects a step forward toward a doctrinal penetration . . . in conformity to the authentic doctrine . . . which should be studied and expounded through the methods . . . of modern thought.

23   *GS* 44.

24   CTI, *Faith and Inculturation* III, 23–26.

25   E. Schillebeeckx, *Church: The Human Story of God* (London: SCM, 1990), pp. 36f.

26   CTI, *Faith and Inculturation* II, 24.

27   A. Ngindu Mushete, 'L'inculturation du Christianisme comme problème théologique' in A. Ngindu Mushete et al. (eds), *Combats pour un Christianisme Africain* (Kinshasa: Faculté Théologique Catholique, 1981), pp. 11–12.

28   Paulo Freire, the Brazilian educationalist, has written of this revolution in pedagogy: *Pedagogy of the Oppressed* (Harmondsworth: Penguin, 1972).

9

MYSTAGOGY AND CHRISTIAN FORMATION

MYSTAGOGY AND EVANGELIZATION

In the Old Testament the word *bśr* means 'to proclaim good news'. An event was announced and that event preceded news about it. Revelation was through deeds first: the wonderful works of the Lord – Exodus, Creation, Covenant – let the God of Israel be known to those who were able to grasp the significance of these events. Interpretation and communication of these events came later. The proclaimer is related to the divine source of the good news so closely that the proclamation becomes an act of cult. The prophet is anointed 'to bring good tidings to the afflicted . . .' (Isa 61:1).[1] In the New Testament, Jesus takes these words and makes them integral to his own proclamation of God's Kingdom as he brings good news of the expected last time (in Luke 4:18):

> The Spirit of the Lord is upon me, because he has anointed me to preach good news to the poor. He has sent me to proclaim release to the captives, and recovering of sight to the blind, to set at liberty those who are oppressed.

The Good News proclaimed by Jesus is also related to deeds, to his saving acts – above all to his death, resurrection and sending of the Spirit. Jesus' life was a revelation, in human terms, of God's love, caring, healing and preferences. For his followers, the Good News was the story of Jesus' life and mission, the coming of his Kingdom through the action of the Spirit. Not abstract 'truths' but concrete events are the content of the apostolic preaching. The Good News was something which happened to change people's lives for the better – in some way that they could easily grasp.

Christian parents are the first mystagogues for children baptized in infancy. It is they and members of their household who lead to early experience of the divine. The example of faith in action makes a first and lasting impression.

In our own times, for the document which was fruit of the Synod on evangelization, *Evangelii Nuntiandi* (1975), 'Evangelizing is in fact the grace and vocation proper to the Church, her deepest identity. She exists in order to evangelize . . .'[2] This emphasis on evangelization is marked by the themes and thrust which produced the Second Vatican Council: awareness of the failure of the Good News to reach modern man and woman, and of the Church's part in that failure due to outdated methods and a theological language no longer accessible to people of contemporary culture.

The RCIA makes the precatechumenate a period (*tempus*) of evangelization, one of the four periods into which the initiation is divided:

> The . . . precatechumenate . . . is a time of evangelization: faithfully and constantly the living God is proclaimed and Jesus Christ whom he has sent for the salvation of all. Thus those who are not yet Christians, their hearts opened by the Holy Spirit, may believe and be freely converted to the Lord and commit themselves sincerely to him . . .[3]

In so far as clear categories can be traced in early times, the patristic distinction seems to have been between a *kerygma*, which is the announcing of the Good News to pagans, and *catechesis*, which has the characteristic of handing on the deposit of the faith in a complete way to new members of the Church.

Pope Paul's *Evangelii Nuntiandi* insists on the need to evangelize cultures, on the renewal of humanity, on integral liberation as a part of evangelization, and on the Kingdom of God, which is a social reality, situated in history, as well as being eschatological.[4] Pope John Paul's mission encyclical, *Redemptoris Missio* (1990), also treats of the Kingdom of God in the context of evangelization and sees the incarnating of the Gospel in the cultures of peoples as a part of the Church's mission.[5] In the perspective of the building up of the Kingdom of God, the struggle for the transformation of social, economic and political structures must be seen as part of evangelization.[6]

In our world, become a 'global village' through communications, no atemporal philosophical god may substitute for the Lord Jesus Christ, incarnate, through us, in the world of today. Like it or not, evangelization is conditioned by our witness, not just on the micro scale of individual acts of love, but also and perhaps above all, on the macro scale of world structures which witness to or against the Kingdom Jesus came to found. Jesus came as Good News to the poor, Liberator of captives and Proclaimer of a Jubilee Year of remission of debts (Luke 4:18). This programme for Jesus' public life is intrinsic to the Christian Mystery: his death was connected with his stance on matters political, economic and cultural, as well as those strictly 'religious'. The mystagogic initiation of peoples to discipleship of Jesus today cannot abstract from the social aspects of the Mystery.

CATECHUMENATE AND CATECHESIS

The word 'catechesis' comes from the late and rare Greek word *katēchein* which is not found in the Greek (Septuagint) translation of the Old Testament, but is found in the New Testament, especially in St Paul. Its primary meaning is 'to resound from on high', but it can also mean 'to instruct', to teach someone. Paul uses the word in the sense of 'giving an instruction on the content of faith'. It is thought that, in preference to the more usual expression for teaching – *didaskein* – Paul may have chosen the word *katēchein* as a technical term for the imparting of specifically Christian instruction.[7]

The later tension between presenting a Christian religion which is primarily mystery, or one which is first of all doctrine, did not arise for Paul. Indeed, most of the patristic period saw an organic preaching which respected the totality of the biblical message, and only emphasized elements of doctrine when these were threatened. The Church was young and catechumens numerous; the surrounding culture had not been permeated by the Gospel, so that the central mystery had to be presented constantly to new candidates – and to Christians whose faith was less than secure.

Over the centuries, the intellectualizing of the Christian message, through the adopting of Greek philosophy as an instrument for understanding and systematizing, drew catechesis into the doctrinal orbit. The secondary place given to the Bible in theology was mirrored in catechesis. Experience, even the most 'religious' experience, that of mysticism, was not thought relevant to the standard religious formation of the young or of catechumens. The dogmatic age had dawned and lasted more than a thousand years. When the early erroneous versions of the Christian message had been successfully dealt with – it was to combat them with their own weapons that Greek philosophy was introduced into reflection on faith – theology had become a scientific discipline in its own right and gradually began to hold its head up alongside the growing number of secular academic disciplines.

So supreme was the hegemony of an intellectual type of catechesis that scholars of antiquity, coming across mystagogy and seeing that it was linked to baptism, classified it under catechetics. Many distinguished patristic scholars of this century speak of 'Mystagogic Catecheses' in the case of Cyril of Jerusalem, John Chrysostom and Theodore of Mopsuestia.[8] Others see that there is a problem about this designation for the Eastertime homilies, especially since the title of 'Mystagogical Catecheses' for the mystagogic homilies of Cyril of Jerusalem does not seem to be original, and at the end of the first of the five he himself speaks simply of continuing with the *mystagogies*, without any mention of catechesis. Others again, opt clearly for calling these discourses simply 'Mystagogies', or 'Mystagogical Instructions'. The translators, from the Syriac manuscripts, and editors of Theodore of Mopsuestia admit that *they* chose the title *Catechetical Homilies*, which is not in the original, because it fitted the diverse matter and allowed them to group together 'Explanations' on the Credo, the Sacraments and on the Church; and in order to fit the style of presentation adopted by the author.[9]

This erroneous classification did not help towards an understanding of the true nature of mystagogy and its traditional role in religious formation. That wrong classification, and the rationalists' aversion to anything to do with mystery of religion or mysticism, account for a good part of the failure to recognize the positive values of mystagogy in modern times.

After a lapse of many centuries (apart from 'mission lands', where it had been reintroduced earlier, but often in an ambiguous form), the catechumenate was revived, by decree of Vatican II. In the *Ordo* for the Christian Initiation of Adults (RCIA), catechesis received a new impetus and was given, once more, a place in the overall context of Christian initiation.

On the one hand, catechesis is little mentioned in the RCIA, which tries to give full value to the *total experience of initiation*, and not just to an intellectual 'learning of catechism'; on the other hand, the recognition by the Church of the importance of initiation has, in fact, given catechesis a new lease of life; after all, catechesis was the reigning structure for all religious formation. Catechesis was the only form of 'religious education' known to most Catholics. The RCIA only speaks of catechesis during the catechumenate. For the time of conversion or precatechumenate, the RCIA uses the traditional term 'evangelization'. When speaking of the time after the celebration of the sacraments of initiation, the Latin original of the *Ordo* speaks of 'mystagogy' and does not mention catechesis.[10]

In the RCIA, catechesis forms only one of the four ways in which a 'suitable pastoral formation and guidance' are imparted (*Catechumenatus est tempus protractum, quo candidati institutione pastorali donantur et opportuna disciplina exercentur . . .*). This catechesis is to be:

1. A suitable catechesis . . . gradual and complete in its coverage, accommodated to the liturgical year, and solidly supported by celebrations of the word. This catechesis leads the catechumens not only to an appropriate acquaintance with dogmas and precepts but also to a profound sense of the mystery of salvation in which they desire to participate.[11]

The description of catechesis given here includes aspects of mystagogy, in speaking of leading into a 'profound sense of the mystery of salvation'. The other three 'ways' of this catechetical *tempus* for the catechumens are:

2. . . . A spiritual journey . . . they pass from the old to a new nature made perfect in Christ . . . a progressive change of outlook and conduct . . . [It is here that the catechumens may experience suffering for their new-found faith:] Since the Lord in whom they believe is a sign of contradiction, the newly converted often experience divisions and separations . . .

3. Participation in liturgical celebrations.

4. The exercise of an apostolic life.

Mystagogy is characterized above all by *experience*: 'More effective understanding of mysteries' ('deepening their grasp of the paschal mystery and . . . making it part of their lives') is to come from 'meditation on the Gospel', but also and especially through 'their experience of the sacraments they have received'.[12]

For some time prior to Vatican II, there was a tendency to file all types of Christian teaching under the rubric 'catechesis', giving rise to expressions such as 'kerygmatic catechesis' for the first announcing of the Gospel. More recently, the pendulum has swung in the other direction, and the various forms of catechesis tend to be included under the rubric of 'evangelization': the Apostolic Exhortation *Evangelii Nuntiandi* (1975), fruit of the Third General Assembly of the Synod of Bishops (1974), says of catechetics, 'A means of evangelization that must not be neglected is that of catechetical instruction'.[13] (Pope Paul goes on to imply that catechesis is primarily for the young, but later in the same paragraph sees the need for an adult catechumenate for adults who are not yet Christians.) He gives a description of catechetics:

> The intelligence, especially that of children and young people, needs to learn through systematic religious instruction the fundamental teachings, the living content of the truth which God has wished to convey to us and which the Church has sought to express in an ever richer fashion during the course of her long history.[14]

Evangelization, under the form of catechesis, is to bridge the gap between 'evangelization' and 'sacramentalization'.[15]

The maturing of the faith of adult Christians belongs to catechesis but a catechesis which is seen to be part of evangelization:

> The Church . . . seeks to deepen, consolidate, nourish and make ever more mature the faith of those who are already called the faithful or believers, in order that they may be so still more . . . To evangelize must therefore very often be to give this necessary food and sustenance to the faith of believers, especially through a catechesis full of Gospel vitality and in a language suited to people and circumstances.[16]

Catechesis here appears as systematic teaching in the faith, not merely notional, but 'to form patterns of Christian living'.[17]

The Fourth Assembly of the Synod of Bishops (1977) treated of catechetics; and in the Apostolic Exhortation *Catechesi Tradendae* (1979), which resulted from it, Pope John Paul took back some of the ground claimed for evangelization by its predecessor *Evangelii Nuntiandi* (the move from emphasis on evangelization back to catechesis fitted the programme of the new pontificate):

> The Church has always considered catechesis one of her primary tasks, for, before Christ ascended to his Father after His resurrection, He gave the apostles a final command – to make disciples of all nations and to teach them to observe all that He had commanded . . . Very soon the name of catechesis was given to the whole of the efforts within the Church to make disciples, to help people to believe that Jesus is the Son of God, so that believing they might have life in His name, and to educate and instruct them in this life and thus build up the Body of Christ.[18]

Catechesis deals with Christian pedagogy, but does not explicitly identify its own objective as that of introducing those catechized to the Mystery of Christ. Catechesis is seen as directed towards initiation into the fullness of Christian life, but is itself a systematic teaching of doctrine: knowledge of the Mystery in an intellectual rather than an experiential sense:

> All in all, it can be taken here that catechesis is an education of children, young people and adults in the faith, which includes especially the teaching of Christian doctrine imparted, generally in an organic and systematic way, with a view to initiating the hearers into the fullness of Christian life.[19]

Mystagogy has not yet arrived. It is not mentioned in these important documents. Today, initiation into the fullness of Christian life might be achieved through contemplation of the beauty and harmony of creation – with an ecological bias; or through participating in action for the liberation of marginalized and oppressed peoples so that the image of God in which they were created, and of which they have been despoiled, may shine in their lives. These are aspects of the Mystery of Christ's work for the implantation of the Kingdom which appeal to contemporary men and women.

Instead of starting from doctrine, one may start from experience. Instead of beginning outside the Mystery, with the likelihood of never really penetrating it in a salvific way, one can start from inside the Mystery, through experience. As Cyril of Jerusalem said in his first mystagogical homily, 'seeing is far more persuasive than hearing' (see p. 42 above).

The concrete experience of the *Ordo initiationis christianae adultorum*, which has given rise to lively pastoral groups at parish level – especially in France, Spain, Italy and the US – has helped bridge the gap between catechesis and liturgy. So far, however, the precious riches of mystagogy have not been discovered. Occasionally a writer touches on the topic, but the intuition is not developed in the direction of a fuller spirituality.[20]

Theologically, we are emerging from a dogmatic and entering a pastoral age. The turning-point was the Vatican II Pastoral Constitution, *Gaudium et Spes*, on the Church in the Modern World. Experience of the world in which we live is the starting-point for theological reflection today. The experience is often analysed in faith and compared with some sort of utopian vision of the world as the Creator intended it. In Jesus Christ this vision is named – the Kingdom of God. Theological reflection is, in turn, not simple contemplation of truth – an end in itself – but is directed to action. Pastoral action is planned through decisions aimed at transforming sinful aspects of the situation originally experienced. In work for the Kingdom, Christians can meet non-Christians who also chafe at social, racial, political, cultural and economic injustices suffered by their brothers and sisters. The Church exists for the sake of the Kingdom in whose service peoples of many religions may meet. The Kingdom extends throughout the universe and joins creation in which poets, mystics and ecologically conscious men, women and children have a stake. Experience of any of these facets of the Mystery of Christ, in whom and for whom all things were created (Col 1:15–16), may serve, mystagogically, for the beginnings of Christian initiation.

Examination of the history and components of mystagogy leads to the conviction that it is a great mistake to relegate mystagogy to the status of a final – and almost optional – extra, added on to the 'serious' work of evangelization and catechesis, which (in this schema) would be without any mystagogic content. It is well to recall that for the patristic literature on Christian initiation, insertion into the Mystery is the key to the entire process.

To promote that insertion through religious experience is the role proper to mystagogy. Approaches to the Mystery, as discerned by contemporary spirituality and examined by theology, are many and varied. Religious formation has a correspondingly wide area of experience on which to build, both intellectually and through experience. Experience is the privileged starting-point today.

The (mainly middle-class) movements which have arisen in the Church over the last fifty or sixty years, all have some sort of religious formation in view. Some, like the Cursillos de Cristiandad, provide conditions for a post-baptismal conversion. They have less success with the follow-up. Others, like the 'Neo-Catechumenate', set out to give a full formation to those who, being baptized in infancy, did not undergo a catechumenate prior to baptism. Modern in their use of psychological methods; urban in their specialization; literate in their reliance on lists, manuals, pamphlets and magazines, these and other movements provide religious formation, in some shape or form, for their members: Bible-study, reading of their manual, study of case-histories, seminars, and so on. Some, in fact, use religious experience to great effect to break down the resistance of beginners and to help towards conversion through the example of the conversion-experience of existing members (as in the Cursillo movement). It is a pity that these movements have not discovered the language of mystagogy and its insistence on the unifying centre of Christian life in the one Mystery of Christ.

The religious formation of the non-practising must lead to experience of the Mystery in terms which modern men or women can appreciate and must start from where they stand culturally. Doctrinal teaching will have its place, but that is not the first place, nor the most important. If a name is to be given to the process of formation/recuperation of the faith of these adults, it might well be mystagogy.

As long as religious formation is reduced to the imparting of information about the tenets of faith, the alternative project of a course in 'religion' which would present the distilled essence of all faiths looks plausible. Once the primacy of mystagogy over catechesis is appreciated, that alternative is seen to be absurd. The central Mystery of faith to be experienced in community, through the mediation of symbols, allows of no woolly common denominator of religions.

NOTES

1   G. Friedrich, *'Euangelizomai'* in Kittel, 1-vol. edn, pp. 267–73.
2   *EN* 14.
3   RCIA 9.
4   *EN* 20, 24, 30.

5   *RM* 52.
6   It is this conviction as to what contributes to the building up of the Kingdom which makes the Brazilian episcopate put evangelization as the overall aim of their pastoral effort when formulating the General Objective of Pastoral Action of that Church.
7   H. W. Beyer, '*Katēcheō*' in Kittel, 1-vol edn, p. 422. In the Gospels *katēcheō* and allied words do not appear with reference to Jesus. The word *didaskein*, on the contrary, occurs about a hundred times in the Synoptic Gospels, generally with reference to the activity of Jesus: M. Preiswerk, *Education in the Living Word* (Maryknoll, NY: Orbis, 1987), p. 67.
8   Both Hamman and Daniélou in A. Hamman (ed.), *L'Initiation Chrétienne*, Textes recueillis et présentés par A. Hamman, Introduction de Jean Daniélou (Paris: Grasset, 1963; republished Desclée de Brouwer, 1980); G. Bareille, 'Catéchèse', *DTC* 2 (1905), col. 1888. Dom B. Botte, in his edition of the pilgrimage record of *Éthérie* (47, 1), on p. 261, gives as title of the section 'Les Catéchèses mystagogiques'; Aetheria's own words about the bishop were *exponit omnia, quae aguntur in baptismo*.
9   R. Tonneau and R. Devreesse (eds), *Les Homélies Catéchétiques de Théodore de Mopsueste* (Vatican City, 1949), Introduction, p. 9.
10 RCIA 7d, 37–40.
11 RCIA 19.
12 RCIA 37–38.
13 Pope Paul VI, *Evangelii Nuntiandi* 44. The change in primacy, from catechetics to evangelization, parallels the change in mentality from a Europe-centred Church – with rare conversions, and evangelization left to 'missions' – to a pluralist 'World Church', where structures of mere maintenance are obviously insufficient, and proclamation of the central Christian message is a constant necessity.
14 *EN* 44.
15 *EN* 47.
16 *EN* 54.
17 *EN* 44.
18 *Catechesi Tradendae* 1.
19 Ibid., 18.
20 Cf., for example, R. A. Oakham, 'Sowing for a good harvest: the underpinnings of mystagogy', *Catechumenate* 12 (1990), pp. 22–7.

10

SERVICE AND SPIRIT

Diakonia in the New Testament means, first of all, 'waiting at table', 'providing for physical sustenance', or 'supervising meals' (Luke 10:40; Acts 6:1). A more general meaning is that of discharging a loving service. *Diakonia* is linked with works, faith, love, patience (Apoc 2:19).[1] In Acts there is the anomaly of the choice of the seven to serve at tables – in contrast with the later accounts of the preaching and other activities of Stephen and Philip, two of the seven. The names of the seven are given, but they are never called deacons. Nevertheless, it seems that the function of *diakonia* came from the designation of this service at table.

In the New Testament, the term *diakonia* is used generically to include many forms of ministry, without specifying the service rendered by the deacons. In 1 Corinthians and Ephesians, diverse ministries for building up the body of Christ are included in the word *diakonia*:

> Now there are varieties of gifts, but the same Spirit; and there are varieties of service (*diakonion*), but the same Lord . . . (1 Cor 12:4–5)

> And his gifts were that some should be apostles, some prophets, some evangelists, some pastors and teachers, for the equipment of the saints for the work of ministry (*diakonias*), for building up the body of Christ . . . (Eph 4:11–12)

Theodore of Mopsuestia, in his mystagogic comments on the Eucharist which the neophytes have just celebrated, shows how 'good works' flow from the Eucharist, just as do harmony and peace:

The new birth has made them grow into a single body; now they are to be firmly established in the one body by sharing the body of our Lord, and form a single unity in harmony, peace and good works.[2]

All forms of Christian sanctity include some outpouring of charity – some service of others – some *diakonia*. The glory of God and service of one's neighbour are the two legs on which Christian holiness walks.

The crucial instance of *diakonia* or service of others is that attributed by Jesus to himself. It occurs in the challenging (parallel) passages (Matt 20:25–28; Mark 10:42–45; Luke 22:25–27) where Jesus makes his criticism of the 'pagan' abuse of authority, and the dangers inherent in every exercise of power over others:

> You know that those who are supposed to rule over the Gentiles lord it over them, and their great men exercise authority over them. But it shall not be so among you; but whoever would be great among you must be your servant, and whoever would be first among you must be slave of all. For the Son of man also came not to be served but to serve, and to give his life as a ransom for many. (Mark 10:42–45)

Addressed to his disciples, Jesus' words apply directly to religious power. It is well to recall the warning. In the culture of obedience that in recent years has given way to the culture of experience, great insistence was placed on obedience to superiors of all sorts. The Church looked askance at any form of revolution – no matter how tyrannical the ruler – because 'the principle of authority' seemed to be at stake. Strange to say, obedience to the Word of God was not stressed; care was taken to have even God's Word filtered to subjects through human superiors. Yet, in the Gospels, Jesus speaks more clearly about the dangers of the abuse of authority than he does about obeying human rulers. It is a sad commentary on Vatican II – so liberal in many ways – that the bishops balked at quoting the first verse of the Synoptic passage given above. Mention of Jesus as giving his life to serve was acceptable, but in the fifteen or more places where the later verses of the passages are quoted (using all three Synoptic Gospels), never once is the first verse included, the one which speaks of the rulers of the Gentiles making their authority felt in lording it over their subjects, and which condemns the 'pagan' style and abuse of authority.[3]

The letter to the Hebrews joins love to service, coupling *agapē* with *diakonia*:

> For God is not so unjust as to overlook your work and the love which you showed for his sake in serving the saints, as you still do. (Heb 6:10)

Commenting on this passage, C. Spicq remarks that since Christ has placed himself at the service of men (Matt 20:28; Luke 22:26–27), the word *diakonia* has taken on, under the New Alliance, a religious and cultic significance.[4] Not only for those in authority, but for all followers of Jesus, service of others is a necessary parallel to service of God. Mystagogy, to be complete, must introduce the neophyte to this *diakonia* which forms part of Jesus' own understanding of his mission and his Mystery.

It is one of the 'discoveries' of contemporary theology that to oppose love of God and love of fellow men and women is to create a false opposition. Vertical and horizontal are not opposed, except in the mind of ideologues: in the experience of work for the construction of the Kingdom they meet. Where so-called 'horizontal' values are really achieved, and men and women gain life in greater abundance, the Kingdom is being built up. 'Horizontal' action for the betterment of this world could only be seen as separate from concern for God's glory as long as theology dealt in an 'eternal' way with static truths formulated in the categories of Greek philosophy. Once an action-oriented theology began to see work for the Kingdom as embracing the political, economic and cultural (as well as individual) living of virtue, the transformation of this world – human beings fully alive – became inseparable from the pursuit of God's glory.

The Church, too, is at the service of the world: in the opening pages of *Gaudium et Spes* the Church as a whole, like Christ, comes into the world not to condemn but to save – not to be served, but to serve.[5] The final paragraphs of the Pastoral Constitution repeat this theme as an inclusion or closing bracket to the whole document:

> Let us pattern ourselves daily more and more after the spirit of the Gospel and work together in a spirit of brotherhood to serve the human family which has been called to become in Christ Jesus the family of God's children.[6]

This Vatican II theme of the Church as Servant was the basis for one of the 'Models of the Church' suggested by A. Dulles, in a celebrated work of the same title. Thus 'The Church as Servant' joins the Church as Institution, the Church as Mystical Communion, the Church as Sacrament and the Church as Herald in the list of models or images of the Church in contemporary ecclesiology.[7] Of this model of the Church as Servant, Dulles says:

> The Church's mission, in the perspectives of this theology, is not primarily to gain new recruits for its own ranks, but rather to be of help to all men, wherever they are. The special competence of the Church is to keep alive the hope and aspiration of men for the Kingdom of God and its values. In the light of this hope the Church is able to discern the signs of the times and to offer *guidance* and

prophetic criticism. In this way the Church promotes the mutual reconciliation of men and *initiates* them in various ways into the Kingdom of God.[8]

In this passage, Dulles uses the expressions 'guidance' and 'initiate', which belong to the vocabulary of mystagogy. In exercising its role as Servant, the Church is acting as mystagogue: the service of leading men and women – contemporary society – into the sphere of the Kingdom of God initiates them into the Mystery of Christ and is a mystagogic service. The Church is seen as at the service of the growth of the Kingdom of God – a perspective shared by *Lumen Gentium*.[9] The expression 'prophetic criticism' is also important. It reminds us that the condemnation of all that blocks the coming of the Kingdom is part of the service that the Church renders to humanity.

In a recent work on ecclesiology, E. Schillebeeckx speaks of the Church as a witness to Jesus' way towards the Kingdom of God, through service:

> The church is not the kingdom of God, but it bears symbolic witness to that kingdom through its word and sacrament, and in its praxis effectively anticipates that kingdom. It does so by doing for men and women here and now, in new situations (different from those in Jesus' time), what Jesus did in his time: raising them up for the coming of the kingdom of God, opening up communication among them, caring for the poor and outcast, establishing communal ties within the household of faith and serving all men and women in solidarity.[10]

To help the poor and outcast break their bonds for the coming of the Kingdom is a service or *diakonia* leading them into the heart of the Mystery of Christ; it is a *diakonia* that is, at the same time, mystagogic.

The present age, pastoral rather than dogmatic, tends to bridge the gap between theory and practice. It is in experience that theory and practice are harmonized and this is an age of experience rather than of abstract principle. The pastoral approach to theology starts from experience and aims at more effective action. Truth consists in finding the true way – the way that leads to life: Jesus presents himself as convergence of way, truth and life, 'I am the way, and the truth and the life' (John 14:6). This understanding of truth links it to right action – action that opens the way to life, that follows the leading of the Spirit of life.

In early Christian times, discipleship of Jesus was sometimes known as the 'Way', known to us notably in Acts 22:4, where Paul describes himself as persecuting this 'Way' to the death. In the *Didache* and *Letter to Barnabas*, early catechesis employs the allegory of the 'Two Ways', derived from Jesus' teaching in Matthew 7:13–14:

Enter by the narrow gate; for the gate is wide and the way is easy, that leads to destruction, and those that enter by it are many. For the gate is narrow and the way is hard, that leads to life, and those who find it are few.

Once more, 'life' is linked to the way which leads to it. Pastoral truth consists in finding the true way of life, in practice and not just in theory. Orthopraxis is taking over from orthodoxy. In Jesus' time and in Hebrew culture, the two were scarcely opposed.

The service or *diakonia* that Christians render aims at the construction of the Kingdom for which Jesus came on earth, died and rose again. The Kingdom that Jesus preached from the beginning is presented again, after the resurrection, as the reason for his earthly career: in the opening verses of Acts, Luke depicts Jesus as 'appearing to them during forty days, and speaking of the kingdom of God'. Paul, whose mysticism leads him to present (evident especially in the dubiously Pauline letters to the Colossians and Ephesians) Jesus' work in terms of the Mystery hidden in God from all eternity, also uses the term 'kingdom of God', 'kingdom of Christ', or 'kingdom of his (God's) Son', throughout his letters, notably in 1 Corinthians (4:20; 6:9, 10; 15:24, 50).

The Kingdom is social and situated in history. It had its prefiguring in the Old Testament People of God – a social and political reality with its own history – and is to have its eschatological realization at Christ's Second Coming. While it spans time and eternity, the Kingdom has its realization in history also – and finally in the Apocalyptic New Jerusalem – bridging the abyss between human handiwork and God's definitive intervention. Human labour is directed towards the building of the Kingdom, yet is constructive only in collaboration with the divine design. The 'commerce' involved in God's taking on a human face means that human labour, as human procreation, is done in creative partnership with God. Necessary now to the coming of the Kingdom, intelligent human effort is not in competition with the Creator, but in partnership. Stewardship of creation is one aspect of this.

A biblical, rather than a philosophical, view of the Spirit helps understand the role of the Spirit in mystagogy and avoid the error of 'spiritualizing'. The Greek philosophical division of things into *spirit* and *matter* is not helpful in this context. Substituting a philosophical for a theological view of spirit has been at the root of misunderstanding of the role of the Spirit in the Church for too long already. To identify the 'non-material' with the domain of the Spirit is the error in question. Because the immaterial or incorporeal is sometimes called 'spirit', it is easy to conclude that to be spiritual means getting away from the material. This theological error owes more to pagan Greek philosophy than to the Bible and has, for centuries, distorted the image of

Christ and of things Christian in the lives of many,[11] and led to the Manichean current which runs through much of Christian thinking since the third century.

The Holy Spirit is responsible for the work of creation, hovering over the waters at the beginning (Gen 1:2), and for the incarnation of the Son of God, coming upon Mary at the Annunciation (Luke 1:35). Each of these works is bound up with matter as well as with God. In fact, it might be said that the drawing of the material into the sphere of God is a task of the Spirit. To avoid the dichotomy of 'matter' and 'spirit' is not easy, so vitiated is our Western culture by the distinctions of Greek philosophers. Once more, it is in experience that intellectual dualisms are overcome. The concrete experience of the incarnation is precisely the harmonizing of Spirit and matter.

Unlike much of the spirituality of his time (the first half of the nineteenth century), the experience-based spirituality of Francis Libermann did not place an abyss between the action of the Spirit in the Christian and his or her inner experience. In fact, Libermann seems to have come to grips with his own epileptic condition through his docility to the action of the Spirit which he discerned with such acuity. Other masters of the spiritual life – especially since the development of psychiatry – try to make a clear-cut division between spiritual direction and psychiatric treatment. Again, it is in experience that the dichotomy between theory and practice is best resolved.

The Spirit is at work in religious experience. The revival of charismatic experiences in groups at prayer is evidence enough of this. I say advisedly 'charismatic experiences in groups at prayer', because the charismatic is an integral aspect of Christian life and prayer since the beginning and not the brand-name of any group or movement. If charismatic experience was muted during centuries, this was an impoverishment of Church life. It is to the credit of the Charismatic Renewal that those involved rediscovered this dimension of Christian life. It would be a mistake to think that on this account they have some sort of monopoly of the charismatic or that the 'movement' (which rightly claims not to be a movement) has said the last word on renewal of the charismatic in the Church for our time.

The Charismatic Renewal insists on the experiential in religion and is convinced, as was John Wesley, that exclusively rational arguments will not produce conversions. Charismatic groups expect individual religious experiences during their meetings and provide a collective experience through a climate of prayer, praise and peace. If some participate in the hope of experiencing the extraordinary, that is a motivation to be corrected in the light of Paul's reminder that charity is the supreme charism (1 Cor 12:31 – 13:13) and that all charisms are destined first for the service of the community – to build it up – and only secondly for the benefit of the individual. It is perhaps a weakness of the Renewal that it has retained its initial format, rather than seeking to be dissolved in enhancing the charismatic element in every Christian gathering. The over-formal style of our current Roman liturgy is sign enough of the need for an infusion of the charismatic. The model should be the community meetings of apostolic times where there is evidence that the exercise of the various gifts was normal.

Contemporary Orthodox theology sees the Spirit as the great Mystagogue, leading Christians, as Christ promised, into the fullness of truth (John 16:13), and initiating us into the Mystery of Christ. The theology of the image of God in the faithful and love of icons go together for Orthodox Christians. It is the work of the Spirit (in baptism) to make the image of Christ emerge radiant from our dark depths, so that Christ being formed in us, we grow to the fullness of maturity in him.[12]

People of the industrialized world live in an overwhelmingly urban culture where the holistic patterns of earlier times remain an almost forgotten memory. Wholeness has become once more a dream for the future. Separation of function is the urban rule, and to some extent this is unavoidable in religion too, but this does not mean that liturgy (the eucharistic celebration above all) should be coldly rational, rather than warmly participative. The present style of ministry contributes to the problems of liturgical celebration, but even while this lasts, much could be done to enhance the charismatic, experiential and mystagogic side of liturgy. If and when charismatic groups give good guidance to newcomers in prayer and discernment they exercise a mystagogic function. Contemplative religious who begin participating in charismatic prayer groups have been known to say that never had they encountered mystical prayer at so deep a level. The community experience of prayer seemed to leave the participants open to the gifts more easily than individual practice of contemplation, even though this latter had been pursued for many years and monitored by spiritual direction. The Spirit seems to be more accessible today in community than in individual prayer – even the most personal, and the shared experiences of members sometimes serve as mutual spiritual direction.

Besides charismatic groups, other modern Church movements give an important place to religious experience. The impact style of retreat, which is the kernel of the Cursillo de Cristiandad, constitutes a powerful religious experience which is produced with the help of modern techniques of persuasion. Other middle-class urban lay movements similarly use banners and badges, the cult of charismatic founders, rule-books, hymns and formation courses to produce religious experience, much as religious orders and congregations have always done. These movements often produce a depth of religious experience that older institutes of religious life no longer offer. Each of these modern movements and associations has its own mystagogy – its own way of introducing members into the Mystery of Christ –

and indeed, its own version of what is important in that Mystery.

Dynamism and the power to act belong to the Spirit of God. To combine reflection and action, as do basic ecclesial communities, and take full account of experience there is need of a spirituality and a theology that give due place to the Spirit. Docility to the action of the Spirit is the key to experiencing the Mystery of God. Passivity is a condition for the Spirit to act and is not inimical to service of the Kingdom.

The fruits of the Spirit – love, peace, joy . . . – precede, accompany and follow action which has the Spirit for guide. The pastoral method of 'see, judge, act' is the setting and not the substitute for discernment of the action of the Spirit. Pastoral planning is primarily theological, in the deepest sense of seeking creative harmony with the action of the Spirit of God. It is a type of planning that is as much mystical as technical. It aims at effective service of the coming Kingdom, neither usurping what belongs to the Spirit, nor denying responsible human partnership in that service.

The creative openness required by docility to the Spirit, in the service of the Kingdom, cannot be legislated for. Spirit, not letter, is the tone of the pastoral age. For a Church long geared to law and letter, this demands a conversion, not only of individuals, but also of structures. When experience takes over from obedience as cultural imperative, the moral authority of pastoral effectiveness largely replaces the formal authority of rank; listening prepares for, and often replaces, teaching. On the mission, the missionary is the first who must be converted. The structured people of God, together creating a history which is to be salvific for many, replaces an authoritarian hierarchy which hands down decisions to inferiors. The creeping 'christo-monism', which looked to the past instead of the future, emphasized authority rather than co-responsibility, and things intellectual instead of experience, begins to be balanced by a theology which is trinitarian in practice and which leads to living in the Spirit.

A new age – that of the Spirit – is taking over from a more 'scientific' and analytic one. There is a tendency to unite holistically, instead of dividing scientifically: synthesis and mysticism are in the ascendant. The whole of creation, over whose birth the Spirit brooded, receives due respect and is seen as fraught with energy. Disparagement of 'animists' may diminish as nature is placed on the agenda for mystics once again. The Mystery of Christ includes all that he embraced in his incarnation – the political and social as well as the individual. Spirituality is seen, not as a denial of matter, but as an enhancing of life and of all that leads to it. Courage in facing the future is a fruit of pastoral discernment based on realistic contemplation of the present. Missionary ardour replaces timid maintenance as characteristic of communities living by the Spirit.

Access to God is through experience of the Spirit active in the community, not through discursive reasoning, psychological plumbing of one own depths or closeness to creation. These other ways may lead to knowledge of some god of the philosophers, but not to the Father of Jesus Christ.[13] For conversion the same holds true. The privileged places of religious dynamism in the Christian tradition are those where an experience of the Spirit is central: Pentecostal Churches, basic ecclesial communities and charismatic and other groups tuned to religious experience. The wider ecumenism, promoting dialogue between the great world religions, sees love for the poor, the despised and the outcast as meeting place for religious people of all faiths. Love and mysticism, each bringing experience of the work of the Spirit, bind people together, while doctrinal straining of gnats separates them. 'Convictions divide people more than doubts',[14] especially in times of change.

Experience of the Spirit is not confined to extraordinary manifestations of charismatic gifts. These latter, while legitimate and positive, are no substitute for charity. The extraordinary is suspect, as it was in St Paul's time, because it can be counterfeited, or coexist with less admirable forms of conduct.

The most striking manifestation of the Spirit in community today, especially in communities of the poor, is action that goes beyond the ordinary capacity of the members. When poor, illiterate, and racially and culturally despised people, who have had no sense of their own worth, begin to unite in solidarity to recover their birthright of children of God and full human persons, something outside the ordinary operations of human effort is at work. This is happening in much of Latin America and in parts of Africa today. The people concerned attribute the change in themselves to the Holy Spirit, or at least to the Word of God, or prayer, because current theology scarcely allows them to think of it as due to the operation of the Spirit.

Sociological analyses of communities of the poor and marginalized show them to be 'pre-modern' and thus irrelevant as agents for the transforming of society – incapable of the sort of political organizing required for changing the contemporary world. The phenomenon of networks of such despised communities uniting in solidarity for their own liberation through the change of political, economic, cultural and social structures, and achieving some little success in their efforts, is a work of the Spirit that confounds the wisdom of the sociologically wise.

The Spirit is given for the completing of the work of Christ in his Body which is the Church, and in the world, wherever the same work of building up the Kingdom of God is undertaken. Christ's lordship, fruit of his Paschal Mystery, is revealed by the Spirit in action undertaken for the transformation of the world. As they become aware of the structured nature of the sin which holds so many children of God captive, Christians and others work to change sinful structures and create solidarity. Joy, peace and strength are palpable in communities which seek in Christ the way out of dehumanizing situations and into a world of justice, peace and respect for creation.

As happens in the hermeneutic circle, it was the experience of the action of the Spirit in Christian communities today that drew attention to the experience of that same Spirit in the New Testament communities. Similar experiences today made the descriptions in the Acts of the Apostles give out a familiar echo.[15]

Prompted by interest in 'Baptism in the Spirit', as popularized by charismatic groups across the spectrum of Christian Churches, a recent book studies New Testament and patristic evidence on the topic of experience of the Spirit in baptism. The authors conclude that the early paradigm for the baptism of converts to Christianity was the baptism of Christ in the Jordan. This model of baptism was current until late in the fourth century. The baptism of Jesus was a trinitarian occasion: the Holy Spirit was seen to descend visibly on Jesus, while the voice of the Father declared him Beloved Son. The Spirit and the gifts of the Spirit were intrinsic to the event and Jesus was seen to receive gifts of healing and wisdom from the Spirit of the Father. Loss of this perspective on baptism had serious consequences.[16] His baptism in the Jordan was Jesus' initiation, at which his identity as Son of God was established and his new life of service began. It introduced experience of the Trinity to the followers of Jesus. The accounts given in the Gospels of the baptism of Jesus 'are about more than just the Jordan event. They are also about Christian baptism.' The study in question holds that 'the central reality of baptism is the imparting of the Spirit'.[17]

Individual 'charismatic experiences' have been recovered in recent times, in the typically 'modern' form of specialized groups set up for this – rather than as a normal constituent of all ecclesial assemblies, as in early times. The fact that whole communities can have an experience of the Spirit is less well known. That the Spirit-led action aims at transforming society, this is new; it is the distinguishing note of basic ecclesial communities. This new form of *diakonia* parallels group effort towards the common good outside Christian milieux.

As Comblin points out, since the Middle Ages the Church has come to occupy, in many ways, the place which belongs theologically to the Holy Spirit. It is the Church which has been seen as communicating to Christians the riches brought by Christ from the Father: God reveals himself through Christ and Christ is known through the Church, that is, through the hierarchy of the Church; the Holy Spirit remains as helper to the hierarchy in communicating Christ; for linking the faithful to Christ, the Church suffices. In Western theology, the Spirit had become unnecessary. Communication, in this case, was thought of as sacramental and 'automatic', or doctrinal and within the competence of those who were commissioned to teach. Religious experience was not considered.

During the centuries when the Spirit was practically in exile from the Church and prophecy at a discount, it was artists – poets, musicians, dramatists – who largely offered the only prophetic service of analysis, condemnation and exhortation to society. Some religious men and women, notably the founders of institutes of common life, performed a similar function; they suffered for this, just as did their secular brothers and sisters. Now that, after a brief season in which the ministry (*diakonia*) of prophecy was once more recognized, it is again being left to artists and other non-canonical persons to keep the creative and critical flame of the Spirit alive in the world, for its salvation.

Experience of God which leads to initiation into the Mystery of Christ, while being action to transform the world in constructing the Kingdom, is an area where the Spirit is seen at work today; it too merits the name mystagogy.

NOTES

1 H. W. Beyer, '*Diakonia, Diakonos*' in Kittel, 1-vol. edn, pp. 154–5.
2 Theodore of Mopsuestia, *Baptismal Homily* 5, 13: E. Yarnold, *The Awe-Inspiring Rites of Initiation* (Slough: St Paul, 1972), pp. 246–7.
3 Luke places this warning of Jesus, and the disciples' dispute as to which of them should be the greatest, immediately after the Last Supper (22:24–27).
4 C. Spicq, *Agapè dans le Nouveau Testament* 3 (Paris: Gabalda, 1959), pp. 65–7.
5 *GS* 3.
6 *GS* 92.
7 A. Dulles, *Models of the Church* (New York: Doubleday, 1974/Dublin: Gill & Macmillan, 1976), pp. 83–96.
8 Ibid., p. 91 (italics added).
9 *LG* 5.
10 E. Schillebeeckx, *Church: The Human Story of God* (London: SCM, 1990), p. 157.
11 Rosemary Ruether, in *Gaia and God* (London: SCM, 1992), has some apt remarks in this connection: 'Good and evil need to be seen as different kinds of relationships, rather than different kinds of "beings" . . . Fundamentalists, however, typically reify good and evil. They treat good and evil as though these were opposite substances, ultimately embodied in opposite cosmic principles, God and Satan. They imagine that it is possible, through some combination of right belief and behaviour, to align oneself absolutely on the one side, disassociated from and purified of all contact with the other' (p. 82).
12 B. Bobrinskoy, 'Mystagogie trinitaire des sacrements' in A. M. Triacca and A. Pistoia (eds), *Mystagogie: Pensée liturgique d'aujourd'hui et liturgie ancienne* (Rome: Edizioni Liturgiche, 1993), p. 30.
13 J. Comblin, *The Holy Spirit and Liberation* (London: Burns & Oates/New York: Orbis, 1989), Introduction.

14 P. Hebblethwaite, *Paul VI, First Modern Pope* (London: HarperCollins, 1993), p. 13, referring to Pope Paul's supposedly Hamlet-like streak.

15 J. Comblin, *The Holy Spirit and Liberation*, chapter 1, on 'The experience of the Spirit'.

16 K. McDonnell and G. T. Montague, *Christian Initiation and Baptism in the Holy Spirit* (Collegeville, MN: Liturgical Press, 1991).

17 Ibid., pp. 243–4.

CONCLUSION

Experience the Mystery – the meaning of the title may now be clear – a mystagogic invitation to savour the Mystery of Christ in holistic fashion.

What emerges from our look at the history and vicissitudes of mystagogy in its various aspects? There is no denying the place it had in the past. But does that mean that it has a place today? Has the *Ordo* for the initiation of adults given adequate future to this ancient practice? The conviction that it has not was the reason for this book.

The case for a real revival of mystagogy today – rather than for the ritualistic and formal recovery which has been the fate of the RCIA version – is bound up with the rethinking of theology which has been under way since Vatican II. In the Scholastic system there was little need of anything not quite rational. Those who are happy with the perpetuation of that approach to the Christian Way will scarcely miss mystagogy. Ironically, it is Catholics who have little time for theological renewal who are members of the new groups and movements that emphasize experience. They may not theorize much about this – they are not given to theorizing – but their practice incorporates religious experience as a high priority. If only they knew it, mystagogy is made for them.

A renewed mystagogy cannot remain exclusively in the hands of Catholics who, though modern in organization and urban outlook, do not have a social conscience. Integrated religious experience neglects no facet of this world and necessarily includes human stewardship of creation and social responsibility.

Mystagogy has tended towards the arcane and backward looking – taking its measure from patristic usage. It needs to become relevant as an instrument of pastoral action in today's world. We need a hermeneutic that helps us discover the pastoral significance of mystagogy for Churches with a largely disenchanted membership, facing problems of hunger, racism, sexual discrimination or economic dependency. What Chrysostom or Ambrose said is important, but what is its significance for young people with no experience of God in their lives, as the third millennium dawns? The past can contribute to the solution of pastoral problems, not through the simple repetition of its texts, but through a hermeneutical rereading of these in the light of the questions of today. In the present, pastoral age, unless theology (and this includes liturgical theology) can clearly be seen as at the service of pastoral effort to change the world, it is largely meaningless.

To provide an experience of Jesus Christ in his Paschal Mystery, to help Christians live that Mystery and dedicate themselves to building the Kingdom, is a chief pastoral work in our time. Both experience and collaboration in building up the Kingdom of God are priorities in contemporary theological understanding and pastoral aim.

Ancient mystagogy had a similar overall aim, but the cultural context was different and the ramifications of the Christian Mystery relevant to the times even more so. Enrico Mazza identifies the purpose that the Fathers who treated of mystagogy had in common: differing in theology and in details of their understanding of mystagogy, they:

> shared a common purpose: to give the baptized the understanding and motivation that will enable them to live the life in Christ that has been bestowed in them in the liturgical celebration. To this end, the Fathers develop a theology of this liturgy wherein the new life of the neophytes has its origin.[1]

Part of the reason for this study is the conviction that mystagogy is better suited to the task of giving understanding and motivation to the baptized than many paths currently being pursued. The other reason is that, at this cultural moment, the experiential nature of mystagogy equips it singularly well for the initiation of adults into the Mystery of Christ and Christian living.

Contemporary industrialized culture is strong on experience and weak on obedience to abstract norms and principles. Traditional cultures, which still flourish in Third World countries, never lost their holistic taste for experience. This cultural constant means that mystagogy is now, once more, for every part of the world, a particularly opportune pastoral practice. It has more to offer than the very limited role conceded it in the *Ordo* for the Christian Initiation of Adults. It should lend its colouring to the entire process of initiation and not be confined to a final chronological stage. The centuries-long hegemony of an intellectual catechesis has so conditioned religious educators that any new approach requires to be highlighted and underlined. Such a 'new' approach is mystagogy, but the *Ordo* has neither highlighted nor underlined it. The English translators of the RCIA, classifying it as catechesis, have effectively sabotaged whatever appeal of novelty might have accompanied the introduction of mystagogy for their parts of the world. Catechetics, the systematic teaching of the content of faith, has long been striving to break out of the bonds of a narrowly doctrinal view of Christian belief; it is not easy to see how it can do this while retaining the name which has for so many centuries been associated with this style of religious formation. A distinct style of religious formation which pays due respect to experience could provide much of what dissatisfied RE teachers are looking for. Such a new style of formation should be called by its traditional name of mystagogy.

Much of the lack of interest in 'religion', as a subject, whether in secondary school or university, is bound up with the fragmentation of the content of the teaching. The division of the intellectual 'content of faith' into so many truths to be learned and believed, or so many rules to be kept, soon dries up the innate curiosity or good will students may bring to the subject. The powerful and unified centre provided by focusing on the one Mystery of Christ overcomes much of this atomization. When this centre is not a truth to be learned, but a burning core to be experienced, the whole exercise changes character.

Mystagogy, as an approach to religious formation, has great potential for drawing pastoral forces together. Already the RCIA has brought catechetics closer to liturgy. Mystagogy, as a style of religious formation and a vital element in liturgy and spirituality, could bring liturgy, catechetics, homiletics and spirituality together in a way which would strengthen all of them. An obvious meeting ground is Christian initiation. Pastoral planning – required of all dioceses by the Synod of 1985 – will bring all aspects of pastoral effort into the unity of a common aim, under effective co-ordination. This process will be helped if various branches of pastoral activity have already begun to reflect and work together.

Mystagogy could well become the term used for introducing into an experience of the one Mystery of Christ those who have already celebrated one or all of the sacraments of Christian initiation, perhaps when they were too young for the celebration to have been meaningful for them. The term would be more in keeping with tradition than those currently in use. On the other hand, mystagogy should bring the experience of the Mystery into every stage of Christian initiation, from evangelization onwards. It should permeate RE for children in a role not less important than catechesis.

If this book helps to show a better way to catechists it will have justified its existence. At least in the industrialized world, they are unfairly blamed for not having transmitted 'the Christian message' to a younger generation. At present, such transmission is an impossible task – a 'Catch-22' situation. The content and understanding of faith of an older generation, yesterday's message in yesterday's language, is not an adequate answer to the problems the young face today: the young reject their parents' version of the Christian message as irrelevant to the world in which they live. Yet, when teachers attempt to provide religious instruction relevant to the times they come up against another problem: children are not suitable subjects for the type of conversion needed in order to embrace a version of the faith different from that of their parents.

Adult religious formation is a priority today. Adults alone are fit subjects for a total religious experience and teaching that prepares them to live Christian lives in today's world. Such experience, for those who only received yesterday's catechism, amounts to a conversion. If they undergo such a conversion, parents will transmit much of it to their children by guiding them into something similar. The task of leading adults into a transforming experience of the Paschal Mystery is mystagogic. Mystagogues as well as, or rather than, catechists are required today.

The new, holistic vision of things, which is emerging out of the bankruptcy of an exaggerated rationalism, is richer in synthesis than in analysis. Analysis was typical of the rational, scientific approach of the Enlightenment. Its shortcomings are now being discovered and new syntheses are popular. It is in this spirit that the chapters of this study have included more than was promised by the chapter headings. Liturgy has received a brief treatment in the chapter (5) explicitly devoted to it, but liturgy permeates nearly every topic discussed in the other chapters, too. Similarly, although having chapters dedicated to them, experience, evangelization and catechesis, initiation, community and the Word of God, crisscross one another throughout the whole book. This organic approach is closer to the oral pattern of communication than to scientific discourse. In the oral mode, now returning to vogue, discourse goes round and round a topic, looking at it from different angles, rather than analysing it systematically piece by separate piece. If this appears as less than scientific, it may also appear as doing more justice to things in their organic totality.

Specialists have not given us any overall introduction to mystagogy. How could they, since the topic is notoriously inter-disciplinary? It is pastoral interest that prompted the present unearthing of the historical, catechetical and other aspects of the theme. The aerial view which results from this survey is necessarily hazy. It is to be hoped that the resulting imprecision in detail, in specialist fields, may be compensated for by the panoramic vista opened up.

The book has, necessarily, the limitations imposed by the attempt to weave together strands of different origins: patrology, spiritual theology, catechetics, liturgy, pastoral theology. I trust that the overall pastoral aim will make specialists who feel that their area of expertise has received less than justice in these pages indulgent towards the attempt. May its shortcomings prompt them to get to work to correct imbalances and fill in lacunae. As G. K. Chesterton insisted, anything worth doing is worth doing badly. The important thing at present seems to be to bring to light the still hidden riches of mystagogy: cutting and polishing may follow.

NOTE

1   E. Mazza, *Mystagogy: A Theology of Liturgy in the Patristic Age* (New York: Pueblo, 1989), p. 165.

INDEX